The Wooden Horse

Eric Williams, M.C.

ARMADA

First published in 1949 by William Collins
First published in this revised junior edition in 1955
This Armada edition published in 1989

Armada is an imprint of the Children's Division,
part of the Collins Publishing Group,
8 Grafton Street, London W1X 3LA

Copyright © Eric Williams. 1955

Printed and bound in Great Britain by
William Collins Sons & Co. Ltd, Glasgow

Contents

Phase One

Introduction

This is an adventure story of the Second World War. It is my own story, but to make it more vivid I have told it as fiction and used the names 'John' and 'Phil' for my friends, Captain Michael Codner, M.C., R.A., and Flight-Lieutenant Oliver Philpot, M.C., D.F.C., R.A.F. I have called myself 'Peter.'

It is some years now since I wrote THE WOODEN HORSE, and even longer since the events described in it took place. In re-reading it to make this special edition, it seems to me scarcely believable that a mere plywood box could have fooled the Germans for so long. Nor does it seem possible that I, or my younger self, could have crossed wartime Germany as I did, knowing so little of that country or its language.

How the escape was contrived and how much of it I owe to the resourcefulness and courage of my companions you will discover in the book, but before I begin my story I would like to describe the prison camp.

The barbed-wire compound, because of its very simplicity, was an extraordinarily difficult nut to crack. In the stone castle or other fortress, the prisoner could always cherish the possibility of secret rooms, underground passages or even sewers. In the simple rectangular barbed-wire cage, there were no such possibilities.

Stalag-Luft III was typical of hundreds of these compounds which the Germans had made all over Europe to keep the prisoners of their early rapid advance. Later, when the Allies had prepared themselves and were fighting back, the Germans took fewer captives, and these, mostly aircrew shot down over enemy territory, were collected in this one enormous camp.

The camp was set in a clearing of the pine forest. The flat grey surface of the compound was broken only by the squat wooden huts raised on piles above the ground to discourage tunnelling. Round the huts the double twelve-foot fence of bristling barbed wire, strong and heavily interlaced, was guarded by high wooden sentry towers which the prisoners called goon-boxes. There were two guards, or goons, in each box, connected by telephone to the main guardroom at the prison gates. They were armed with machine-guns and searchlights which swept the camp continually during the hours of darkness. Between the sentry towers were arc lamps suspended from poles above the wire, while below it, sunk deep under the ground, were seismographs which recorded in the guardroom the vibrations caused by tunnelling.

Outside the wire fence, sentries armed with rifles patrolled between each pair of watch-towers. At night, when the prisoners were locked in their huts, these guards were doubled, and savage police dogs, occasionally visible in the searchlight beams, roamed the deserted compound.

Fifteen feet inside the main fence was a single strand of barbed wire twelve inches above the ground. This was the trip-wire, and anyone stepping over it was shot at by the guards. A narrow pathway trodden by the feet of the prisoners ran round the camp just inside the trip-wire. The camp was so crowded that it had become a convention to walk only in an anti-clockwise direction round the circuit.

The surface of the compound was a mixture of sand, powdered leaf-mould and dirt, which in the summer formed a thick layer of soft dust. In the winter this dust was churned by the prisoners' feet into a grey sea of clinging mud.

Under this top layer the subsoil was clean hard yellow sand; yellow when damp, but drying to a startling white-ness in the sun. The Germans knew that every tunnel carried its embarrassment of excavated sand and viewed each disturbance of the grey upper layer with suspicion. Every excavation made for a drain, rubbish pit or garden was carefully watched by the ferrets, or security guards. It was only by elaborate camouflage that the tell-tale yellow sand could be hidden in these places.

The skin of grey dust formed one of the most effective defences of the camp.

ERIC WILLIAMS

Chapter One

The Daily Round

It was early morning. Inside the room everything was hushed; the eerie, impermanent lifelessness of a room where everyone is sleeping. On the four two-tier bunks ranged round the walls the prisoners slept rolled like cocoons in their blankets. On the table in the centre of the room, softly illuminated by the light that crept in under the closed blackout shutters, lay in disordered heaps the clothes of the sleeping prisoners. Thinly, from the direction of the Kommandantur, came the sound of a distant bugle call.

In one of the upper bunks a figure stirred, grunted and turned over on its back. It lay still for a while; then with a convulsive jerk that shook the whole room it sat up, rubbed its eyes and yawned. Peter Howard, lying in the bunk below, opened his eyes. A few scraps of wood shavings dislodged from the mattress above fell slowly down and rested on his face. He brushed them off, turned over and pulled the thin grey blanket tightly round his ears. It was too early to wake yet. He closed his eyes. He knew it all so well. A pair of legs covered with long sandy hair would appear over the side of the bunk above. Legs that would wriggle their toes disgustingly as their owner prepared to land like an avalanche beside his head. He had seen it all too often before. He tensed himself expectantly. Crash! Bang! Ger . . . doyng! The whole hut shook. One of the shrouded figures moved impatiently and swore in an undertone. A stool slid noisily

13

across the floor. The man who had cursed pulled the blanket up over his head. Heavy footsteps stamped across the room. A short silence, then clang! as the lid of the tea-jug was banged down. Another short silence and then the sound of a spoon being stirred violently inside a pottery mug. Presently the whole room shook again as the door was slammed.

Peter relaxed and slowly opened his eyes. He knew exactly what had happened since the first convulsive thrashing of limbs had jerked him from his sleep. First Bennett had pulled on his socks, then his wooden clogs which had spent the night resting beside his head. Next he had leaped for the wooden stool, missed it and sent it slithering across the floor. He had looked surprised and stamped over to the tea-jug to see if the next-door stooge had fetched the water. Finding the jug contained only a handful of dried tea he had again forced an expression of exaggerated surprise and had filled a mug with cold water from a large pottery jug which stood near the stove. He had added a spoonful of lemonade powder and stirred violently. After drinking the mixture in three great gulps he had gone out, slamming the door after him, to walk round the circuit until breakfast-time.

Every morning since they had arrived at Stalag-Luft III Peter had awakened to the same abrupt reveille. At first he had opened his eyes at the preliminary crash. Now he kept them closed until after Bennett had left the room.

All was silent again. Not a sound from the other six occupants of the two-tier bunks. Either they were asleep or grimly hanging on to the last shreds of slumber until the storm had passed. Bennett had gone now. He would be walking round the compound – just inside the wire – leaving the others to gather together the ragged edges of their slumber. Peter often wondered what Bennett found in prison life attractive enough to get him out of bed so early. Most of them lay in bed as long as possible, reluctant to begin another day. Bennett was a strange chap. Starting the day half an hour before everyone else and then sleeping on his bunk all afternoon. Perhaps he was right. The camp would be deserted at this hour of the morning. Bennett needed plenty of space all round him. He was too bull-like, too virile to live cooped up with seven other people. He needed wide open spaces and a job of work to do. Peter wriggled himself more comfortably into his mattress of wood shavings and tried to sleep again.

From the corner of his right hand came the mumbled ends of Robbie's morning hymn of hate . . . 'Blast, what a noisy devil that fellow Bennett is.' There was bitterness in it, and finality. They would quarrel soon. Peter could see it coming. Starting over some small detail it would flare up into a violent feud. One of them would move into another room and life would go on. It was like that in the prison camp. A man would stand the boredom for so long and then, slightly at first, the personal habits of one of his seven companions would begin to wear him down. Little things such as the way the man ate, or possibly his accent. Life with him would become unbearable.

Poor old Robbie, he had been a prisoner for nearly three years; and a flimsy wooden hut was not Bennett's ideal background. He couldn't have been silent in a padded cell with a thick cork floor. Peter sighed. The thought of a cork floor made him think of bathrooms. He hadn't had a bath for two years – unless a length of hosepiping and a punctured cocoa-tin could be called a bath – and he lay thinking of porcelain baths in all the colours of the rainbow. Green, yellow, pink, black . . . No, he didn't like black. He liked a bath that lent its colour to the water. Green was the best. A green bath, darker green tiles on the wall and a cork floor. Or perhaps a sunken bath. Yes, a sunken bath . . .

He forced his mind away. What about this tunnel?

There must be a place to start one if you could only think of it. David had nearly got away with it. David with his blue seaman's eyes and halo of rosy-red beard. David the farmer. Good old dependable David. David who ran a farm on paper. Over his bunk there was a rough book-shelf made from bed-boards, the narrow cross planks of the two-tier bunks. All the books were about farming. At the right time of the year David would sow his crops and in due course he would harvest them. He kept a profit and loss account. Funny how seriously he took it. If it rained on the day when he had decided to reap he would walk about with a face like thunder. If during a heatwave one of the others remarked on the fine weather he would mutter something about the crops needing rain. Good old farmer David, he was compensating for his imprisonment. But he still tried to escape. He was the room's representative on the Escape Committee. And yet his farm was very real to him.

The only man who knew more about farming than did David was Bennett. But Bennett knew more about every-thing than anyone else. Bennett the authority. Bennett the bull. Full of 'bull'. You couldn't discuss anything with Bennett in the room. No matter what the discus-sion Bennett would finally deliver himself of a categorical authoritative pronouncement which would kill the topic dead. Abortive attempts would be made to revive it but under the weight of authority behind the pronouncement the opposition would languish and finally relapse into a baffled and disgruntled silence.

They were always arguing. Paul caused a lot of the trouble. Tall and thin, so tall that you wondered how he had managed to fit into the Hurricane in which he had been shot down early in the war, he had gone straight from school into the R.A.F. His whole world was flying and the wide freedom of the sky. Paul found prison life more irksome than did most of his fellow prisoners. It

16

tried his patience beyond endurance and it was in these times that he turned to Robbie for consolation.

Robbie was the peacemaker.

Peter forced himself into wakefulness. It was his turn to be cook. Of all the chores of prison life cooking was the one he hated most. It had been harder for the early prisoners. They had had to cook on wood fires in the open air. He had a stove. At least, he had a hundred-and-twelfth share in a stove. There were fourteen rooms in the hut. Each room had eight prisoners and for every eight men there was one cook. At the end of the hut stood a cast-iron stove with one cooking ring and a small oven. Fourteen dinners for eight had to be cooked on that stove every evening. He began to think about the evening meal. If he peeled the potatoes and put them on about ten o'clock . . . His thoughts were interrupted by Robbie.

'What about a spot of tea, Pete?'

'O.K., Robbie. Just going. Bags of time yet.' He stretched and rolled out of his bunk. ''Morning, Nig!'

''Morning, Pete.' Nigel Wilde and John Clinton slept in the bunks nearest the stove. Like most advantages in prison life, this had its compensating disadvantages. Although warmer in winter it meant that the bunks were used as seats during the daytime. Peter preferred the colder privacy of the wall farthest from the stove.

Nigel lay on his back in the upper bunk, his right arm curled round the top of his head. His right hand was gently stroking the left-hand side of his moustache. His expression was blissful.

Peter stood watching him. Nigel winked.

'Why do you keep doing that?' Peter asked.

'I like it, old boy. Feels as though someone else is doing it.'

'You're crazy.'

'I know, it's nice.'

In the bunk below, John Clinton lay dreaming, his dark head resting on a folded pair of trousers, a seraphic expression on his face.

'What's the weather like?' Nigel asked.

Peter padded over to the window. It was late spring and across the wire he could see the pale fronds of a silver birch graceful against the dark olive background of the pine forest. Peter was fond of that silver birch. He had tried to paint it in all its moods. As a sharp but twisting and fragile silhouette against a winter sky. And as he saw it now, a cascade of delicate green, almost yellow in the morning sun. He had painted it often but had never been able to capture its isolated beauty, its aloofness against the darkness of the pines. Overhead the sky was clear and still, the hushed expectancy that foretells a burning day. Under the window the sand was moist with dew, and dew sparkled on the barbed wire. The rows of long green-painted barrack huts looked washed and cool.

'It's a lovely morning, Nig.'

'*Gut zeigen*. What about a cup of tea?' Nigel specialized in translating air force slang literally into German. '*Gut zeigen*' was his way of saying 'good show'. In the same way 'bad show' became '*schlecht zeigen*', and 'fair enough' '*blond genug*'. When he was particularly morose he considered himself to be '*gebräunt weg*', or 'browned-off'. He sometimes used this peculiar German on the guards and was genuinely surprised when they didn't understand.

Peter, still looking out of the window, saw Bennett come striding furiously round the circuit. Wearing heavy army issue boots, a woollen skull-cap and R.A.F. battle-dress, he came past the window at full speed.

'Come on, Pete,' Nigel called. 'What about the tea?'

Peter crossed to a wooden shelf over the stove and took down seven mugs. The tea-jug had been left just inside the door the night before with a handful of tea-leaves in the bottom. It was the turn of the cook in the next mess to

18

take both jugs across to the kitchen and have them filled with boiling water. It would be Peter's turn tomorrow. He poured three mugs, one for Nigel, one for Robbie and one for himself. He would not waken the others yet. There was still plenty of time.

Crossing again to the shelf, he took from a cardboard box a heavy German loaf; ninety per cent potato meal and a liberal sprinkling of sawdust. A loaf that, if allowed to dry, would split into great fissures and become as hard as stone. The cardboard box had once contained a Red Cross parcel from England. There were dozens of similar boxes littered round the room, holding all the personal possessions of the eight prisoners. Boxes piled on top of the cupboards. Boxes under the beds. Boxes round the stove, filled with brown coal, old potatoes and waste paper. Eight such boxes were delivered to the room each week and yet they never seemed to have enough of them.

He cut twenty-four thin slices. A seventh of a loaf a day was each man's ration. By cutting very thin slices he could make three for breakfast, one for lunch and three for tea. He spread them thinly with margarine from a Red Cross parcel, opened a tin of jam, and breakfast was prepared.

He was still in pyjamas.

'What about a cold shower before breakfast, Nig?'

'*Blond genug*, old boy.' Nigel unwound himself from his blankets.

'O.K. Let's wake John.'

'What? Wake the child? Have a heart, old boy!' Nigel treated John with a teasing respect. Respecting him for his fine intelligence and ready courage; teasing him because of his youth and absent-mindedness. John's mind was always on his books or schemes of escape. So far removed from his environment that Nigel often had to go and find him and bring him to his meals. Nigel loved John and masked his affection under a veil of chaffing and elaborate practical jokes. He called him 'the child' and respected him above everyone else.

'Yes, go on! Wake him up, it'll do him good.'

'Shall I?'

'Yes, go on!' Peter waited for the joke that had amused him every morning for days.

Nigel reached for his latest invention, his latest method of teasing John. This time it was an elaborate waking device. A cocoa-tin suspended by a harness of string hung just above John's head. Through a hole in the top of the tin ran another string suspended on the end of which was a bunch of bent and rusty nails. By pulling rapidly on the centre string Nigel could conjure forth a most satisfactory noise. He pulled the string.

John did not wake.

'I think the loose bed-boards were a better idea,' Peter said.

'Yes, but a bit dangerous.' Nigel grinned as he remembered the last waking device he had invented. A device which had effectively removed the one remaining board which had held John's shaking bed together and had deposited him, complete with mattress, on the floor.

'Come on,' Peter said. 'Once round the compound and then a shower.'

Leaving John asleep they clambered out of the window. It was quicker than the door and quieter.

Once more the room was silent. Robbie lay lazily flapping at the flies that were doing circuits and bumps inside his bed space. There was the whole room for them to fly in and they had to come and buzz round him. He gave it up and pulled the blanket over his head. Presently a figure in one of the upper bunks began to curse.

'What's the matter, Pomfret?' Robbie lowered his blanket.

'Oh, it's those two noisy blighters. They're much too

hearty. What do they want to take a cold shower at this hour for? And that tin can thing. It's too silly.'

'Keeps them happy, I suppose.'

'Well, it shouldn't. They shouldn't be happy in a prison camp. Nobody should be happy in a prison camp. It's not decent. And talking of decency, I suppose they're going to sunbathe in the nude again. The S.B.O. ought to stop it. It shouldn't be allowed.'

'Why in heaven not?' Robbie asked.

'It's not decent,' Pomfret said.

'Oh, don't be so lily-livered. I shall sunbathe myself when the weather gets a bit warmer.' Robbie pulled the blanket over his head and lay thinking of the play he was producing. The feminine lead was the trouble. Young Matthews had played it in the last four shows and the audience were getting used to him. He might ask Black. It was the very devil, this feminine lead. So many chaps were shy of taking it on. He'd go round and see young Black later on and try to persuade him to do it.

'Come on, show a leg!' It was Peter and Nigel returned from their cold shower. 'Breakfast up, *appel* up! *Appel* in ten minutes. Who wants breakfast in bed?'

Pomfret rolled out of his bunk, rubbing his eyes and growling under his breath. Putting on a Polish army greatcoat over his pyjamas he took a cardboard Red Cross box containing his washing materials from a shelf above his head, and shuffled off to the washroom.

'What's the matter with her this morning?' Nigel asked.

'Oh, she's a bit touchy this morning,' Robbie told him. 'You woke her with your infernal machine.'

'That's more than I did to the child. Hey, John, wake up! On appel bitty, mein Herr!'

'He's all right,' Robbie said. 'He'll have breakfast after appel.'

In the far corner David Bruce lay thinking. He was

21

planning his day. He was going to drench his new calf. It was not doing so well. To lose a calf now would be a serious thing. Make a hole in the little reserve of capital that he had accumulated.

The door was flung open and a German guard entered the room. '*Raus! Raus! Ausgehen! Alle rausgehen!*'

'Goon in the block!' Paul stood by his bunk, trousers in his hands, hair on end, still in the lower school. '*Deutschland kaput!*'

The guard shouted at him in German.

'Buzz off!' Paul said. 'We don't understand German here.'

The guard shouted again in German; a long sentence that ended with the English word 'cooler.'

'You're for it,' Robbie said. 'It's the cooler for you.'

The guard shouted again. He was nearly screaming now.

'Buzz off!' Paul made his stock retort.

The guard began to unsling his rifle. The bayonet was fixed.

'Better be careful,' Robbie said.

A Feldwebel came walking down the centre corridor of the barrack hut. The guard sprang to attention and made a long, involved complaint in German. The Feldwebel turned to Paul.

'You have been impertinent again, eh?' He spoke in English.

'I object to being shouted at.'

'Come!' The Feldwebel was used to this sort of thing.

Paul finished pulling on his trousers. He was no stranger to the cooler. He was almost happy there. He felt that he was carrying on the fight. He gathered up his blankets and his toilet things and accompanied the Feldwebel down the corridor.

'*Ausgehen, alle rausgehen!*' the guard shouted, unmoved by his victory.

'*Gut zeigen*, Joe. Just coming.' Nigel said it quietly.

22

'Hi, John! On appel bitty! Come on, you'll be late for appel.'

John opened his eyes. He looked blank. Suddenly he realized what it was all about. 'Give me a cup of tea, somebody!'

Peter handed him a cup of tea. John swallowed once and handed it back. He rolled out of his bunk and stood putting on his clogs, a lean brown figure with a mop of black hair like an Abyssinian warrior. His pyjama trousers which had been cut short above the knee were of a different pattern from the jacket, which had no sleeves. The jacket had blue stripes and the trousers had once been pink. He took another gulp of tea, hurled a blanket round his shoulders, snatched up a book and shuffled off to roll-call, a slice of bread and jam in one hand and his book in the other. Once on appel he stood reading his book, taking occasional bites at the slice of bread and jam.

Outside the barrack the prisoners stood in fives. Peter stood next to David who, pipe jutting from the depths of his red beard, puffed clouds of smoke into the cool morning air.

'Why do we always stand in fives?' Peter complained. 'It used to be threes in the last camp.'

'These are air force goons,' David said. 'The others were army goons. Army goons can only count in threes.'

The guards walked down the rows counting them; the guards in uniform, the prisoners huddled under blankets or defying the morning air in pyjamas or shorts. Slowly the guards walked down the ragged lines, counting as they walked. *Drei-und-fünfzig . . . vier-und-fünfzig . . . fünf-und-fünfzig . . . sechs-und-fünfzig . . . sieben-und-fünfzig . . .*

The British adjutant called them to attention. The Lager Offizier, tall and immaculately uniformed, was mincing across the square to where the Senior British

Officer was standing. After saluting the S.B.O. he turned to the assembled prisoners, and bowing from the waist saluted and shouted '*Guten Morgen, meine Herren!*' The Kriegies replied with an incoherent roar. While the more prudent replied '*Guten Morgen, mein Herr,*' the wilder spirits chanted their single-syllabled reply of derision; the two replies combating one another and resulting in an enthusiastic greeting which made the Lager Offizier beam with pleasure. He was popular with these wild-looking British, was he not?

After appel Nigel returned to his bunk. He was plotting his post-war career. He had already decided to be a doctor, a game warden, a gold prospector, a holiday camp proprietor, a farmer (he dropped this almost immediately under the scorn of David Bruce), a big game hunter and a bookmaker. He took one course of study after another, dropping each one as another more attractive career caught his fancy. He lived in a frenzy of enthusiasm – but nothing lasted for long with him.

Peter lay on his bunk waiting for John to finish his breakfast. 'Parcels tomorrow,' he said.

'Good show!' John spoke through a mouthful of bread and butter. 'We'll have the last tin of salmon for dinner tonight.'

'Don't burn it this time,' Bennett said. 'If you'd only do it the way I told you. You want to cover the top with greased paper.'

John said nothing. It was too early in the day to start an argument.

'If we get any raisins we'll swop them for biscuits,' Peter said. 'Then we can make a cake.'

'We'll bake it in the afternoon,' John said, 'and then if it turns out to be a pudding we can have it for dinner.'

'And if it turns out to be porridge we'll have it for breakfast,' Robbie added.

'I wouldn't mind running a restaurant after the war,'

Nigel said. 'Run it for a bit, and then leave a manager to look after it. Then I could start a small farm and supply the restaurant from the farm. The waste food from the restaurant would do to feed the pigs and . . .'

'Sort of perpetual motion,' John said.

'And then when I'd got the farm running I could put a bailiff in that and start on something else.'

'You have to know something about cooking to run a restaurant,' Bennett said. 'Judging by your last effort you wouldn't last long.'

'Farming's a job for the expert,' David said from out of his misery. 'You can lose a lot of money. I've got a calf now that's doing very badly. It's a Friesian. The book says they're difficult to rear. I wish I'd decided on Herefords.'

'Friesians look nicer,' Peter said.

David snorted.

When the others had finished their breakfast Peter collected the eight knives and mugs – they had no plates – and took them over to the washhouse to clean them.

Outside the washhouse was a long queue of prisoners waiting for their morning shower. The camp, which housed nearly a thousand men, possessed six cold water taps. Two of them had been converted by the prisoners into rough shower baths. The remaining four supplied all the water for washing clothes and crockery and for cooking. The Germans had agreed to build shower baths. They had been building them for nearly a year. The unfinished structure stood inside the camp surrounded by its own wire barrier to prevent the prisoners from stealing nails and odd pieces of timber. They had long since given up any hope of using the showers.

Squeezing his way past the crowd of bathers, Peter entered the washhouse. It was full of men washing dirty clothes on long wooden benches; dipping them in water, laying them on the benches, soaping them, and scrubbing them with nail brushes. In one corner several men were trying to wet themselves under the meagre trickle of water falling from the cocoa-tin shower. In the opposite corner a prisoner stood on the wash-bench, his face pressed to the window. All over the camp there were similar figures, watching through holes cut in the walls of the huts, hiding under the huts, peering through half-open doors, spying on the German guards. Every subversive activity in the camp had its nimbus of stooges. Every ferret who came into the camp was shadowed by a stooge, his every movement was reported to the duty pilot who sat at the main gates of the camp.

In the middle of the floor was a dark, gaping hole about two feet square, cut through the six inches of solid concrete on which the brick floor was laid. Next to the hole lay the trap. Built of solid brick on a wooden frame, it could be lowered into position by means of hooks fitting into slots in the sides of the frame. Once the trap was in position and the joints made good with soap mixed with cement dust, it was impossible to tell that the floor had been disturbed. Head and shoulders out of the trap stood a man named White.

'Hallo, Bill,' Peter said.

''Morning, Pete.'

'How's it going?'

'Piece of cake!' White lifted his hand, palm open, forefinger touching the tip of his thumb, and made a clicking noise with his tongue. 'She's doing fine.'

'How far have you got?'

'About forty feet.'

'Ferret approaching!' It was the stooge calling urgently from the window.

White was down the hole in a flash and the trap was lowered on top of him. A crowd of bathers and washers of dirty linen surged over the trap, swamping the floor, camouflaging the trap. Peter set to and washed his crockery, while a running commentary on the guard's progress came from the watcher at the window. The German passed without entering the washhouse and work on the tunnel was resumed.

When Peter returned to the hut he found Bennett 'tin-bashing'. The prisoners were forced to cook in utensils of their own making. Nothing at all was provided by the Germans. The usual thing was a flat dish about twelve inches long by eight inches wide and two and a half inches deep. It was made by taking both ends off a Klim tin and rolling the cylinder into a flat sheet. When a number of these sheets had been collected they were joined together by folding the edges one over the other and filling the joints with silver paper salvaged from cigarette packets. A blunt nail was used as a punch and a narrow groove punched along the double thickness of metal. The edges of the flat sheet thus formed were turned up and the four corners folded to form a dish.

Bennett, surrounded by pieces of rolled-out tin, was bashing furiously, bashing the tin with a personal vindictiveness that made the hut shake and the tins rattle on the shelves.

'It's a lovely day,' Peter offered.

Bennett grunted.

'Wouldn't you rather do that outside in the sun, old boy? Besides, the hut wouldn't shake so much if you bashed on the sand.'

Bennett grunted again.

Peter sighed. He put the crockery and breakfast cutlery on the shelves and went out to walk round the circuit until lunchtime.

Outside the hut he met Robbie mooching round clad in an old pullover and army slacks cut down to make shorts. The ragged ends of his shorts flapped round his lean brown legs. He was wearing home-made sandals.

'Hallo, Pete. Mail come in yet?'

27

'Not yet, Robbie – it's late this morning.'

'Is Bennett still bashing?'

'Yes.'

'God! I wish that chap would move into another mess. Y'know, he's not like an ordinary man. If he wants to open a door he doesn't just turn the handle. He throws himself at it with all his strength and then when he finds the lock won't break he turns the handle.'

They walked several circuits in silence.

'This is an awful life, y'know, Pete.'

'Yes. Pretty foul. Makes you appreciate life at home though. What wouldn't I give to walk on grass again!' He savagely kicked the sand at his feet. 'There's a place in Warwickshire I'd like to be now, on the Avon. There's a place where I used to bathe, a steep bank where you can dive into a deep pool.' He thought of the sun dappling through the trees on to the river bank and the earthy smell of the brown river, the warm grass under his naked feet. 'I'm going there as soon as I get back to England.'

'I shall go back to my wife and kids,' Robbie said.

Peter kicked a stone that lay on the path in front of him. His feet were bare but hardened. His life before the war seemed long ago, a different life. Softer and less real than the life he was living now. 'I often wonder whether it's better or worse for you married men – imprisonment, I mean. At least you've got something waiting for you and the old shekels piling up in the bank. You've got your life fixed. This is just an interlude for you. I sometimes feel that life is running past me and when I get back it will be too late.'

'Too late for what?' Robbie asked, smiling.

Peter kicked another stone. 'Oh, too late to begin life again . . . It's this awful feeling of time passing. I'm not getting anywhere – not even fighting . . . It's such a waste of time.'

'I'm wasting time too, you know,' Robbie said gently.

28

'My youngest will be two and a half next week and I haven't seen her yet.'

'That's just what I mean, you've got something concrete ahead of you. Something behind you too, to look back on.'

'Well, you can build for the future. Lots of chaps are taking degrees in all sorts of subjects.'

'Yes, I know,' said Peter moodily. 'But I can't settle down to that sort of thing. I'm browned off this morning. *Gebraünt weg*, as Nig would say. I want to escape and get back to England.'

'Bah, escape! How many people have got back from this camp so far? None!'

'But there's no harm in trying,' Peter said. 'It gives you something to do. You're not just sitting down waiting for the end of the war.'

'How long has Bill White's crowd been on the washhouse dienst?'

'Just over two months.'

'And how far have they got?'

'About forty feet.'

'There you are. They've another three or four months' work yet before they're even under the wire. They haven't an earthly, Pete. Not an earthly. The goons are bound to tumble to it before then.'

'Oh, I don't know. People have got out before now.'

'Yes, but what percentage? Out of every thirty tunnels started I suppose one gets through. Once you're outside the camp your difficulties have only just begun. It's no good, Pete. They'll never make it. It's just a waste of time.' Robbie walked on, hands in pockets, head lowered, kicking up the sand of the circuit as he walked. A sharp wind ruffled his soft grey hair and carried the dust from the circuit across the trip-wire. It brought with it the sound of gramophone music from one of the wooden barracks and the smell of burning brown coal blocks.

'What's the time?' Peter asked.

Robbie looked at his watch. 'Just after twelve.'

'Good gracious. It's time I went for the tea water.'

'You've time for another circuit,' Robbie said. 'You can get hot water until twelve-thirty.'

'O.K. I'll avoid the queue then.'

They walked on in the warm sunshine.

'I'd like to get out,' Peter said. 'I'd like to get out even if it's only for a few days. You feel so cut off here. I often wonder if the world's going on just the same outside. I'd like to see a cinema show and use a telephone – how I'd like to use a telephone! And I'd like to go up and down in a lift – and walk on carpets – and climb stairs. I'd like to spend money and have to make a decision.'

'You can make a decision now,' Robbie said. 'What to have for dinner.'

Peter laughed. 'Not even that. Parcels come tomorrow. We've only got a tin of salmon left.'

'Well, you can decide what book to take out of the library – or what socks to wear tomorrow.'

'I can't – I haven't any clean.'

'I wonder you don't cut your feet to blazes.' He looked down at Peter's bare feet.

'Oh, I haven't worn shoes since the winter.' He lifted one of his feet. Its sole was brown and hard as leather. 'Have to get this hard skin off before next winter – I don't think I could wear shoes for long now.'

'There you are,' Robbie said. 'That's a decision.'

'Yes – and here's another. I'm going for the tea water.'

'See if there's a letter for me as you go by, will you?' Robbie said. 'I'll wait here and you can chuck it out of the window.'

'Right.'

He found that Bennett had finished his tin-bashing. The room was empty. Lying on the table were several Kriegsgefangener letter forms. He sorted them out. One

30

for John, two for Nigel, three for Pomfret, one for himself. He crossed over to the window and called out to Robbie. He held out his fist with thumb extended downwards. Robbie shrugged his shoulders and mooched on, hands in pockets.

While Peter and Robbie walk round the circuit Paul is in the cooler. It is a narrow cell high up in the German barrack. It has one small window at the level of the ceiling. The window is covered from the outside by a metal plate which stands a foot away from the wall. A certain amount of air finds its way round the edges of the plate but the prisoner cannot see the sky.

He has had no breakfast. His shoes have been taken from him and even if he had a book he could not read in the dim light of the cell. He knows the cell. He has been here before. He knows that shortly after two o'clock, if the sun is shining, a stray beam of light will enter the cell, creeping in through a small space between the metal plate and the window-frame. He will watch this beam of light. In it specks of dust will be floating, beautiful faerie specks that will dance and swirl in the sunlight as he fans the air with his hand. He will sit looking at them until, with the movement of the sun, the beam of light is there no more.

Presently he hears footsteps in the corridor and the sound of a key in the lock. The door opens and a guard is there with his midday meal. He knows this too. He will have the same meal every day he is in the cooler. A small bowl of cabbage water and two potatoes cooked in their jackets. He sits on the bed while the guard places the food on the table. He likes to treat the guard as a waiter. Physically, he suffers the hardships of solitary confinement; mentally he wins a battle in the constant war against the enemy.

He spends the long afternoon lying on his bunk and

31

thinking of home. He thinks, too, of the barrack room he has just left. In a way, it is good to be in the cooler again, away from the insistent company of his fellow prisoners. He is an individualist, a natural fighter pilot. Not for him the dependence of the bomber crew. He is the lone wolf, alone in the cockpit of his Hurricane, far above the clouds in the blue sky, with the sun above him gilding his wings and turning the fleecy clouds below him into a carpet of snow. His is the lone encounter above the clouds, his prey the full-bellied bombers escorted by the waspish vicious fighters. Two three-hundred-miles-an-hour fighters twisting and turning in the sky. The rattle of machine-guns, and the loser plunging burning into the clouds that wait below.

He imagines himself in the cockpit of his Hurricane (the kick of the controls as you go into a flick roll, the matchless rhythm of a perfectly timed roll off the top, and the way the patchwork quilt of the earth slides over you and the sudden smell of petrol as you pull out of a loop). He remembers the smell of glycol and the way the parachute bumps against the back of your legs as you run out to the waiting aircraft, the bounding over the rough turf, the smoothness as you become airborne, the quick climb through the clouds and the thrill of sighting the enemy below you, silhouetted against the clouds. He remembers the attacking dive when you clench your teeth and press the firing button and the aircraft judders with the firing of the eight Browning guns, the sudden blackout as you pull out of a dive and the quick look round for the enemy as you recover. The slow roll over the airfield before you come in to land, the peace and quiet as you switch off the engine, the smell of the grass as you climb down from the aircraft and the small friendly sounds of the countryside as you stand there smoking a cigarette, waiting for the truck to take you back to the dispersal hut.

He lies thinking of this as the cell grows dark. He

falls asleep lying on his bunk, the shoddy blanket across his chest, his face young in sleep, untroubled, free.

Chapter Two

John Has An Idea

A few weeks later the ferrets pounced and Bill White's tunnel was discovered. These ferrets were ubiquitous in the camp. Clad in blue boiler suits and three-quarter boots, they would be found lying underneath the huts or hidden in the roofs listening for incriminating evidence. They came in and out hidden in the rubbish carts and even climbed in over the wire during the night so that the duty pilot who sat patiently at the main gates could not book them into the camp. Some of the ferrets with a sense of humour would report to the duty pilot as they came and went. There was politeness between them, and mutual respect. It was a constant game of counter-espionage.

The compound was deserted. It was afternoon. Most of the prisoners were sleeping on their beds. Outside the barbed-wire fence the posten paced their beat, their rifles slung high across their backs. Beyond the wire the forest, remote and unreal from inside the camp where no trees grew and the ground was arid and beaten hard by the feet of the prisoners, lay dark and cool beneath a cloud of pale green leaves.

Peter and John walked slowly, hands in pockets, round the circuit of the wire, idly watched by the sentries in the boxes. As they walked they were speaking in low tones.

'Pity about Bill's scheme,' Peter said. 'I thought they stood a chance with that.'

'It was too far from the wire,' John told him. 'Think of all the sand you've got to hide to dig a tunnel three hundred feet long. The only way to get out is to make the tunnel as short as possible – start somewhere out here, near the trip-wire.'

'You couldn't do it. There's nowhere near the wire to start a tunnel from. They chose the nearest building to the wire.'

'Why start from a building at all? Why not start out in the open here – camouflage the trap. We could come out to it every day and take it slowly.'

'But that's impossible. It's like the top of a billiard table. Every spot of ground near the trip-wire is in full view of at least three goon boxes and two outside posten. You couldn't possibly sink a shaft out here. Besides – how would you get the sand away?'

'It was done once. Ages ago by some chaps in another camp. A crowd of them went out with a chap who played an accordion. While he played they all sat round in a big circle and sang. And while they were singing they dug a hole in the middle, passed the sand round and filled their pockets with it. They got the hole as deep as a man's arm, put some boards across it and replaced the surface sand. Then they all went back to their huts with their pockets full of sand.'

'What happened?'

'Oh, a sentry came into the compound that night, walked over the trap and fell down the hole. The whole thing was too slapdash and hurried.'

They walked on in silence. To Peter the idea was new and worth considering. 'There must be a way,' he said. 'All we need is something to cover it with, some sort of innocent activity like the accordion. But we can't do that again – must be a classic by now.'

34

'Might do something like it,' John said.

'I don't know – it's all so bare. If only there were some trees.'

'Goons hate trees.'

'The trouble is you've always got to have such a good reason for anything you do. If we start mucking around with the landscape we've got to show it's for some definite purpose, something quite different.'

'I sometimes get tired of working out goon reactions,' John said. 'All this "we think that they think that we think" stuff. You're so frightfully in the dark.' He shivered and looked up. 'Hallo, look at the trees. There's another of those whirlwind things on the way.'

Peter stopped. Over to the south the tops of the trees were bending and waving while the air in the camp was cold and still. Then sudden gusts of wind came across the camp, catching windows left loosely open, blowing up spouts of sand, snatching at the washing hung on lines outside the huts. The swastika over the Kommandantur flared out suddenly, then drooped again.

'I'm going in to shut the windows,' Peter said. 'Left the food on the table. Coming?'

'I'll stay and watch,' John said.

He shivered again as Peter hurried off. The whole camp had come to life. Prisoners dashing out of the huts and snatching washing from the lines, windows slamming. By now the nearest trees were bowing to the wind and John moved into shelter behind a hut as the fine sand whipped across and stung his legs.

Here she comes, he thought, and quickened his pace, reaching the side of the hut as the whirling column of dust and sand left the trees and swept towards the wire. Leaves and bits of paper were caught up and flung into the air and as he watched a large sheet of newspaper whirled upwards, mounting the spiral, up and up, fifty or sixty feet, floating and staggering; crowning the whirlwind as it hit the camp. The nearest goon box was enveloped in a cloud of sand and John had a sudden impulse to rush the wire while the sentry was blinded.

In a moment it was all over. The fine dust still hung in the air but the sand was gone and the rushing in the trees had fallen to a sigh.

Far away from the camp the piece of newspaper was floating downwards and, as he watched, it drifted on to the tops of the pines, hung absurdly for a moment and then slipped out of sight.

Wish that was me, he thought. I could do with a miracle like that. Like old Elijah. Or the Greek tragedies. *Deux ex machina*. When the plot got stuck you lowered him down in a box and he sorted everything out. He pictured a genial old man with an olive wreath drifting down into the camp and offering him a lift. 'Any more for the *Skylark*? Penny a ride on Pegasus . . .'

And then he found himself running across the camp, an idea racing through his mind. The god in the box – the Trojan horse. Peter – he must find Peter.

He found Peter lying on his bunk, listening to Robbie's latest complaint about Bennett. His eyes were closed.

John tried to appear calm. 'Pete, the wind's dropped. What about finishing that walk?'

'O.K.' Peter was grateful for the interruption. 'Just a minute while I light my pipe.' He took the cigarette from Robbie's hand and held it to the bowl of his pipe. 'I should let it drop, Robbie – you can't do anything about it.'

'I'm getting moved to another mess,' Robbie said. 'If that noisy blighter doesn't . . .'

'Come on, Pete,' John said.

'I'm with you.' Peter handed the cigarette back to Robbie. 'Come for a walk. It'll do you good.'

'The circuit gives me the willies,' Robbie said.

They walked on the firm sandy soil in the circuit. The windstorm had passed leaving the camp clean, scoured. The air was still now and the prisoners were hanging their washing on the lines.

John was trying to appear calm. He was still tense with the excitement of the idea, but he spoke calmly.

'Pete – you know the idea of camouflaging the outside trap?'

'Yes?'

'I was thinking after you'd gone in. You said the last one was a classic by now.'

'Well, it is, in a way.'

'So is this. What about the wooden horse of Troy?'

Peter laughed. 'The wooden horse of Troy?'

'Yes, but a vaulting-horse, a box horse like we had at school. You know, one of those square things with a padded top and sides that go right down to the ground. We could carry it out every day and vault over it. One of us would be inside digging while the others vaulted. We'd have a good strong trap and sink it at least a foot below the surface. It's foolproof.'

'What about the sand?'

'We'll have to take it back with us in the horse. Use a kitbag or something. We'll have to keep the horse in one of the huts and get the chaps to carry it out with one of us inside it. We'll take the sand back with us when we go in.'

'It'll have to be a strong horse.'

'Oh, we'll manage it all right. There's bags of timber in the theatre. You'll be able to knock one up all right.' John could see it already. See it clearly and finished. As a complete thing. The wooden vaulting-horse, the vertical shaft under it and the long straight tunnel. He could see them working day after day until they got the tunnel dug. And he saw them going out through the tunnel.

'Let's go and see the Escape Committee now,' he said.

'There's no hurry. Let's get the whole thing worked out first.'

'We'll go now,' John said. 'Someone else might think of it while we're still talking about it.'

An hour later they were back on the circuit. They had put the scheme before the Committee, who were at first incredulous, then mocking, finally intrigued. They had registered the idea as their own and had been told that if they could produce the vaulting-horse the scheme would have the full backing of the Committee.

'We'll have to get some strong pieces of wood for the framework,' Peter said. 'Four pieces about three inches square and five feet long would do for the legs. Then we've got to have pieces to go round the bottom to tie the legs together – the same round the top . . . And then we've got to cover the sides. I don't see how we can possibly do it.'

'I was thinking of that. Why not cover the sides with canvas?'

Peter considered the idea. 'I don't think that would do, because the sides will have to be solid, otherwise there's no point in covering them at all. And if we do anything pointless the goons will get suspicious and wonder why we've done it. No, this will have to be an absolutely pukka vaulting-horse without anything phony at all.'

'Why not cover the whole of the four sides with bed-boards?'

'No, that won't do!' Peter said it emphatically.

'Why not? We've plenty of bed-boards. All the chaps will give up one or two each.'

'That's not the point. Do you realize what the thing would weigh if we made the sides of solid wood? It would be as much as we could do to lift it, let alone carry someone inside it. No, we'll have to think of something else.'

They walked on in silence, pacing slowly round the wire.

'I've got it, John!' Peter said suddenly. 'There's our supply' – pointing to the unfinished washhouse – 'we'll pinch some of the rafters out of the roof of the new shower baths. Get some nails too while we're about it.'

'We'll have to do it after dark,' John said. 'There's no moon now, let's do it tonight.'

'What about the dogs?'

'We'll have to risk them. The searchlights worry me more than the dogs. I'll dig a sunbathing pit outside the window and we can crawl from under the hut into that. Then if we leave a few benches or chairs lying outside the other windows we can crawl from one to the other.'

'I'm more worried about the dogs.'

'We'll get Tony Winyard to look after the dogs. He'll make a row and attract them down to that end of the camp. What's worrying me is where to hide the wood we get out.'

'Oh – bury it in the sand under the hut or somewhere. When we get it sawn up we can hide it in our beds.'

'O.K. – that fixes the framework all right. But what about the sides? There's not much point in getting the stuff for the framework until we know what we're going to use on the sides.'

'It'll come,' Peter said. 'It'll come. Don't look too far ahead. Let's get organized for tonight. We'll think about the sides tomorrow.'

At dusk each evening the guards came into the compound and herded the prisoners into the huts. From dusk until dawn the prisoners were locked in the huts while outside in the compound the darkness was stabbed and dissected by the searchlight beams which swept the camp continually throughout the night.

39

There was no system in the sweeping of the search-lights. Peter had spent hours sitting at the abort window watching them. At times it would appear that the men on the lights were following a strict routine – one light following the other in its restless movement across the camp. There seemed just time to dash quickly from one hut to another in the interval between the beams. Then, with startling abruptness, the beam would stab out in a totally unexpected quarter, utterly confounding the system.

It was quite dark in the centre of the compound. Round the wire, covering an area of some sixty feet in width, the ground was brilliantly lit by the arc lamps hanging above the wire, a ring of white light surrounding an area of darkness in which stood the blacked-out wooden huts. In each hut, cold and dead from the outside, a hundred prisoners, each with his own private problem, crowded into family intimacy. Each darkened hut seething inside with living cells, loving, hating, chaffing, wrangling.

It was eight twenty-five in the evening. Five minutes before zero hour. In Peter's room the men sat round the table talking nervously. It was like the crew room before take-off. An air of tension and an eagerness to get it started. To get it over with.

During the afternoon Peter had loosened several boards in the floor. The huts stood on wooden piles raised a few feet above the level of the sand. Often during the night Peter had heard the dogs sniffing and prowling about under the floor. He was thinking of this now as he sat, dressed in Australian dark blue battledress, his face blackened with wood-ash, waiting to slip out through the trap he had made.

He was frightened of the dogs. There was something terrifying to him in the thought of the dogs prowling about in the darkness of the compound. Animals trained by men to hunt men. Men themselves were all right. They knew when to stop. But where would the dogs stop if they caught you? He had seen them being trained outside the wire. He had seen them set on the masked and padded 'quarry' by the *Hundmeister*. Seen them bring him to earth and stand over him growling softly. He rubbed his right hand slowly up and down his left forearm and glanced impatiently at his watch.

John sat, a mirror in front of him, smearing wood-ash on his face. 'What time is it, Pete?'

'Twenty twenty-five. Better wait until twenty-thirty before we go. I hope they don't bungle things at the other end.'

'Who's doing it?' Robbie asked.

'Tony Winyard.'

'What's he going to do?'

John was still rubbing wood-ash on his face. 'He's going to crawl out of the bottom hut to attract the dogs up to that end of the camp.'

'Sooner him than me,' Pomfret said.

'And me,' Peter said. 'He's done it several times. He carries a bag of pepper and reckons he can throw it in the dog's face. Sounds rather like putting salt on a sparrow's tail to me. Still, it'll be useful to us if he can keep the dogs up at that end for about ten minutes. They stage it rather like a bull fight. Tony's the matador. The cape-handlers each have a hole in the floor of their room and call to distract the dog's attention. Must be rather funny. The brute doesn't know which way to go.' He looked again at his watch. 'O.K., John. Off we go.'

He crossed to the trapdoor and lowered himself into the darkness under the hut. The sand felt cool to his hand and the air was musty and full of the odour of pinewood. He crawled towards the edge of the hut and lay waiting until John joined him. 'After the next beam has passed,' he said, 'we'll make a dash for the sand pit.'

They reached the sand pit and lay there in its friendly

41

darkness, waiting for the right moment to start the long crawl to the washhouse. It was over a year since Peter had been out of the hut after dark, and he lay on his back looking up at the sky. There were no clouds, and the heavens were trembling with a myriad of stars. He lay there feeling the night air on his face, the cool sand under his hands.

It took them some time to crawl through the wire surrounding the new shower house, but once inside, with the wire replaced, they were free from the dogs and searchlights and could work in peace. They worked fast. There were some long wooden rafters lying against one of the walls and these Peter sawed into suitable lengths with a small hacksaw blade. John searched for nails and any odd tools lying around. He found a bricklayer's trowel and about a dozen good long nails.

When Peter had collected sufficient timber he passed it to John who had crawled back through the wire, and between them they dragged it to the hut.

Several times on the way back they had to lie flat while a searchlight enveloped them in its blinding light. It's just like being over Berlin, Peter thought. Just the same feeling of naked vulnerability.

Once they heard a dog bark; a short sharp yelp of rage that made them grin nervously in the darkness as they squirmed towards the hut.

There was more than the usual noise coming from the hut that night. A carefully orchestrated background to drown the sound of their working. Peter knew that every blackout shutter in the hut was unfastened, that men were waiting in every room to drag them inside should they have to bolt for it.

They gained the hut without being discovered and buried the timber and the trowel in the sand under it.

The next morning Peter went along to the camp theatre

to borrow some tools, while John canvassed the compound for prisoners who were willing to vault.

The camp theatre was a large room formed by removing two of the partition walls in one of the centre huts. A low stage had been built at one end of the room. Behind the stage was a small dark recess used as a dressing-room, property room and carpenter's shop.

For some weeks past he had been helping to construct and paint the scenery for the next dramatic show. It was made up of narrow 'flats' – wooden frames covered with thin brown paper. If the covering of the frames was done on a damp day the paper contracted when the weather changed, and split. If the covering was done on a dry day the paper expanded and sagged. It was the usual thing to paint an entire 'flat' one evening and return the following morning to find it split from top to bottom.

He found McIntyre, the stage carpenter, making easy-chairs from the plywood chests in which the Red Cross parcels arrived from England.

''Morning, Mac,' he said.

McIntyre was a typical stage carpenter, taciturn, pessimistic, and a genius at improvisation. He grunted.

'How's it going, Mac?'

'O.K.'

'I've come to see if I can borrow a hammer.'

'Aye.'

Peter sat back in one of the finished armchairs and looked round the small cluttered room. Mac's retreat. The bulwark that Mac had built himself against the boredom of prison life. Pieces of furniture, machines for 'noises off', properties. All Mac's. He leaned comfortably back in the chair and sighed.

'This is a comfortable chair, Mac.'

'Aye.' (Hammering at one of the chairs.)

'We could do with one of these in our room.'

'Aye,' Mac said. 'I dare say.'

Peter sat up. 'Mac, could you spare me any of this plywood?'

'What for?'

'I want to make a vaulting-horse.'

'A what?'

'A vaulting-horse. You know – one of those box horses. I want to cover the sides with plywood.'

McIntyre straightened up. 'Aye, you'll need quite a number of boxes for that. I'm having a load sent in from the Kommandantur. I'll have some extra ones put in for you.'

'Thanks a lot, Mac. Could you spare me any three-inch nails? I'll get on with making the framework this morning and then I'll be ready for the plywood when it arrives.'

'Aye,' McIntyre said. 'Why the sudden interest in gymnastics?'

Peter dropped his voice to a whisper. 'Camouflage for a hole.'

'Sorry, Pete.' McIntyre's attitude became at once cold and antagonistic. 'I can't let you use these tools for escape purposes. You know that as well as I do. They're on parole. Even if they weren't, you'd mess 'em up. Why on earth don't you give it a rest?'

'O.K., Mac.' He understood McIntyre's jealousy for his tools. His not being able to escape himself and not wanting other people to try either. 'O.K., Mac,' he said. 'I shouldn't have asked you really,' and he started to move towards the door.

'Why not go along and see "Wings" Cameron?' McIntyre said. 'He's got a few illicit tools and he'll lend a hand in making it.'

'I'll go along now,' Peter said. 'Thanks all the same, Mac.' As he walked towards the wing-commander's room he wondered why McIntyre had suggested that. Just to get rid of him, or with a genuine desire to help? How little I know of him, he thought. How little I know of any of them. Old Mac, completely absorbed in his carpentry. Proud of his resourcefulness in making something out of nothing. Making a vocation out of imprisonment.

'Wings' Cameron lived in a small room at the end of Block 64. As a wing-commander he enjoyed the privilege of a room to himself. He needed it. Because he was another enthusiast. And enthusiasts are not easy to live with in a prison camp. He, too, loved making things. Give him a piece of string, some bent nails, a few empty Klim tins, leave him alone for a while and he would produce a lamp, a cooking stove, a patent device for digging tunnels – whatever you had asked him for.

As Peter walked down the corridor of Block 64 he could hear the sounds of hammering coming from the room at the end of the hut. Good show, he thought, he's in the mood for heavy work.

He stopped at the wing-commander's door. Stuck to the centre panel was a cartoon cut from an American magazine. It showed a convict digging a hole in the floor of his cell. He was using a pickaxe. Outside the barred door, over which the convict had draped a blanket, stood two wardens talking. 'I don't know what he's making,' one of them was saying, 'but it's keeping him very quiet.'

Peter grinned and knocked on the door.

'Come in,' called a friendly voice, and Peter entered the cell-like room.

'Wings' Cameron was a small man with a large moustache. A plumber's moustache. He was wearing a pair of Egyptian sandals, rose-coloured socks, a pair of faded grey flannel trousers and a bright yellow shirt with a large red handkerchief of Paisley design knotted loosely round his neck. He had been shot down wearing these strange clothes. 'Thought I'd dress like a foreigner,' he explained later, 'then I shouldn't be noticed if I had to bale out. But I must have dressed as the wrong sort of foreigner, because I was arrested quite soon.'

45

The room was twelve feet by six feet. Across the narrowness of it, at the end farthest from the door, stood a two-tier bunk. The bottom bunk was made up for sleeping. The top bunk was a confusion of old Klim tins, bits of wire, bed-boards, the pieces of a broken-down cast-iron stove, and the remains of a wooden bicycle that 'Wings' had started to make and never finished. Klim tins stood in rows on wooden shelves fixed to the walls. Klim tins stood on the table and on the chairs. Klim tins overflowed all these and stood in serried rows under the bunks. The tins were filled with nails, pieces of string, screws, nuts and bolts, small pieces of glass, odds and ends of paint from the theatre. Everything that 'Wings' had acquired from years of diligent scrounging.

Along one wall, under the window, were fixed a drawing-board and a work-bench. On the drawing-board was pinned a scale drawing of a sailing yacht. On the work-bench lay another confusion of odds and ends, a vice made by 'Wings' out of the parts of an old bed, and a model steam engine constructed from Klim tins and a German water bottle.

As Peter entered the room, the wing-commander was nailing a wooden batten to the floor. The batten formed a frame round a large square hole he had cut in the floor.

'What's that for?' Peter asked.

'To stop me falling down the hole.' The wing-commander replied without looking up from his work.

'No, I don't mean the piece of wood. I mean the hole itself.'

'Oh, that!' He straightened himself. 'That's part of an air-conditioning plant I'm fitting.'

'How will it work?'

'I'm fitting a fan under the floor. I've got the parts of it here.' He pointed to a wheel with propeller-like blades cut from plywood. 'The fan is driven by a belt and pulley from a large wheel under the floor. A shaft runs from the wheel up through the floor to the top of the work-bench. I shall have this old gramophone turntable mounted on the top of the shaft. The winding-handle of the gramophone will be fixed to the turntable as a crank. When the room gets too hot I merely turn the handle and cold air is driven up through the hole in the floor. The hot air leaves through another hole I'm going to cut near the ceiling.'

'Why don't you use the gramophone motor to drive the fan?' Peter asked.

'Oh, the motor's broken. I used the parts to make a clock.'

'Wait till the goons see it. They'll be after you for damage to Reich property.'

'They have.' The wing-commander said it with satisfaction. 'The Feldwebel came round this morning and started screaming at me in German. I told him to push off and bring someone who spoke English. Then a Gefreiter came crawling under the hut and tried to nail the hole up from underneath. I pranced around stamping on his fingers. He went away after a bit and came back with a Lager Offizier. I'm going into the cooler for fourteen days.'

'It's a wonder they don't take your tools away.'

The wing-commander looked cunning. 'Look at this.' He pointed to a tool-rack fixed to the wall over the work-bench. 'Have a look at these tools.'

Peter examined the tools. Every one was phony. It must have taken 'Wings' weeks to fashion the hacksaw blades and wicked-looking knives from pieces of rolled-out Klim tins. There were chisels too, made of wood and painted to look like steel.

'They do a swoop now and again, but all they find is this. All my real tools are hidden behind the panelling of the wall. They think I'm mad, but quite harmless, really.'

Peter laughed. 'I expect they think most of us are round the bend. I want to make a vaulting-horse and I

47

came along to ask your advice and see if you could let me have a bit of plywood and some nails.'

'Yes, I think so.' To him a vaulting-horse was a problem in terms of materials available.

Peter explained about the tunnel. He did not want the wing-commander to be working in the dark. 'Wings' was at once enthusiastic.

'We must set it out first,' he said. He unpinned the drawing of the sailing yacht and replaced it with a sheet of clean paper. 'It will have to be light and strong,' he said. 'Strong both ways. Both for vaulting and for carrying you inside it.' He took up a scale rule and bent over the drawing-board.

Chapter Three

The Tunnel Is Started

Between them they had built the vaulting-horse. It stood four feet six inches high, the base covering an area of five feet by three feet. The sides were covered with two-feet square plywood sheets from Red Cross packing-cases stolen from the German store. The sides tapered up to the top which was of solid wood boards padded with their bedding and covered with white linen material taken from the bales in which the cigarettes arrived from England. There were four slots, four inches long by three inches wide, cut in the plywood sides. When pieces of rafter six feet long and three inches by two inches thick had been pushed through these holes the horse could be carried by four men in the manner of a sedan chair.

The horse was kept in the canteen. A canteen in

name only – a long, low extension to the camp kitchen, containing the barber's shop and a large empty room used as a band practice room. Like all the other buildings in the compound, it was raised above the surface of the ground; but it was built on a brick foundation and more solidly than the living quarters. The entrance was by double doors reached by a short flight of wide wooden steps.

While the horse was being built John had been recruiting prisoners for the vaulting. He had posters made which he stuck up round the camp, advertising gym classes which would be held every afternoon. Special prisoners were detailed to talk to the German guards, remarking on this typical English craze for exercise and telling them, casually, about the vaulting-horse.

Some days later the few afternoon walkers on the circuit were surprised to see the double doors of the canteen open and a team of prisoners dressed only in shorts march down the wooden steps and form up in a line near the trip-wire. They were followed by the four strongest members of the team carrying a box-like object slung on wooden poles. The box was carried to a spot about forty-five feet inside the trip-wire where it was carefully placed on the ground and the poles withdrawn.

The team formed up and under the direction of one of the prisoners began to vault over the box. The guards, bored with watching the prisoners walking the endless circuit of the wire, turned towards the unusual spectacle. They did not give their whole attention to the vaulting. A boxing match or a faked spontaneous fight was a well-known Kriegie method of distracting the attention of the guards while an attempt was being made on the wire. So the guards watched the vaulting but cast an occasional glance along the strip of wire for which they were responsible.

The standard of vaulting was high. The captain of the

team led his men in a complicated series of jumps. Only one of the men was not so good. His approach was clumsy and his vaulting not up to the standard of the others. The guards soon singled him out as the butt of the party and grinned whenever he failed to clear the horse. The vaulting had drawn a crowd of amused prisoners, who jeered and cat-called whenever he made his run up to the box. Every time he failed to clear the horse he drew a guffaw of laughter from the surrounding prisoners.

Soon the guards in the boxes were leaning on their elbows waiting for him to make his run. It was not often they had the chance to laugh at the British prisoners. The boot was usually on the other foot. The more the spectators laughed the more determined this man appeared to be to clear the obstacle. He took a final, desperate leap and in missing his footing he lurched into the horse and knocked it over. He knocked it over on to its side so that the interior was in full view of the guards.

The horse was empty. The vaulters righted the box and went on with their sport. Soon they carried the horse back into the canteen, where they left it until the following afternoon.

Before they left the canteen they tied pieces of black cotton across the doorway and from the edge of the horse to the skirting-board. The following morning the cotton was broken. The ferrets were taking no chances. During the night the vaulting-horse had been examined.

It was after breakfast, a week after the vaulting had first started. Peter and John were walking round the circuit. The subject of their conversation – it had been nothing else for a week – was the vaulting-horse.

'I think we might start digging tomorrow,' John said. 'The goons have got used to the vaulting now. We've knocked the horse over often enough for them to see that there's nothing going on inside. Besides, the chaps

50

who are vaulting want to get some return for their labour. They won't just go on vaulting if nothing happens.'

'Yes, I know, I'm rather worried about the vaulters. It's tough going on the little food we get. How long do you think it'll take us to dig the tunnel?'

'Let's see.' John hitched his shorts with his elbows. 'We've got about forty-five feet to go to the trip-wire, thirty feet across the danger strip. That's seventy-five feet. The wire itself is about eight feet thick so that makes eighty-three feet. We should break at least thirty feet away from the wire because of the outside sentries. That gives us one hundred and thirteen feet altogether. That's if we go straight. Allow a bit for going round rock or tree roots and make it a round figure of one hundred and twenty feet. . . . A hundred and twenty feet. If we do five feet a day it will take us twenty-four days.'

'We shan't do five feet a day,' Peter said.

'Oh, I don't know. I could dig five feet in a day. Make it three feet if you like, that will make it about six weeks.'

'It's not a matter of how much we can dig in a day – it's a matter of how much we can carry away in the horse. Do you realize how much sand weighs?'

'You should know that – you're the construction boss.'

'As far as I can remember a yard of sand weighs about ten hundredweight, but I don't know whether that's wet or dry. Ours will be wet, of course. But knowing that wouldn't help us much. What we want to know is how big a pound of sand looks, so that we can figure out how much we can dig in one session. How much do you think they can carry in the horse – with one of us inside as well?'

'What do you weigh?'

'I don't know. I was eleven-three when I was shot down. I expect I'm about ten-seven or ten-ten now.'

'Then I'm about ten. Supposing we say we can carry ten stone of sand.'

'That's a hundred and forty pounds – let's go and weigh a pound of sand and see how much it looks. I think a foot a day seems more reasonable than three feet.'

'What shall we use as a pound weight? I think a gallon of water weighs about ten pounds.'

'We'll use an unopened tin of Klim – that weighs exactly a pound nett. We'll make some scales, put an empty Klim tin on the other end and fill it with damp sand until the scales are even. Then we'll know what a pound of sand looks like.'

'Right,' John said. 'We can't go in yet. They're holding a Latin class in our room.'

'I suppose I ought to be going to German classes really.'

'Oh, I shouldn't bother. After all, we shan't travel as Germans. A little knowledge is dangerous. If you start learning German now and start talking outside you'll get us both in the cart. Your best role is dignified silence. We'd better travel as Frenchmen and I'll do the talking. As long as you can say *Ich bin Ausländer – nicht verstehen,* that should get you through.'

'O.K.,' Peter said. '*Ich bin Ausländer – nicht verstehen.* Sounds impressive. What does it mean?'

'It means "I'm a foreigner – I don't understand."'

'That seems a good line. I suppose I just keep on saying that until you come along.'

'You can pretend to be deaf and dumb if you like.'

'I know! I'll have a pronounced stutter. Then if they ask me anything I'll just stutter and you interrupt and tell them what they want to know.'

'Yes, I'll do that if they talk French, but if they don't you just stick to the *nicht verstehen* business.'

'Right,' Peter said. '*Ich bin Ausländer – nicht verstehen.*' He walked on round the circuit thinking of the escape. *Ich bin Ausländer – nicht verstehen.* What a vocabulary to try to cross Germany with. But even if I spoke fluent

52

German, how much better off would I be? It's all a matter of luck, this escaping business. Chaps have got through to England without any German at all. And fluent German speakers have been brought back. And that's looking too far ahead too. We've got to get out of the camp first. Let the morrow look after itself. It would be nice to be back in England though. Feeling as though you were doing something instead of stewing here waiting for the end of the war. Back on the squadron with the flying and the fear, and the relief, and the parties in the mess, and the feeling that it could happen to anyone else but not to you. And the feeling of thankfulness the next morning that it hadn't happened to you and that you could go out that night and you wouldn't have to worry again until the night after . . .

That evening Peter made the top section of the shoring for the vertical shaft. He made it with four sides of a plywood packing case reinforced and slotted so that they could be assembled into a rigid four-sided box without top or bottom. The box would stand a considerable inwards pressure.

John spent the evening in making twelve bags from the bottoms of trouser legs. Several of the prisoners had made themselves shorts by cutting their trousers off above the knee. When John had sewn the bottoms together, roughly hemmed the tops and inserted string, the trouser legs had become bags about twelve inches long. He fashioned hooks from strong wire with which he intended to suspend the bags inside the horse.

During the week they had made two sand pits, one at the side and one at the head of where the horse was standing. They had made these ostensibly to soften the shock of landing on their bare feet. Actually they served as a datum mark to ensure that they always replaced the horse on the exact spot.

The next afternoon they took the horse out with John inside it. He took with him a cardboard Red Cross box to hold the surface sand, the trouser-leg bags and hooks, one side of the vertical shoring and the bricklayer's trowel they had stolen from the unfinished shower baths.

This is worse than going on your first 'op,' Peter thought. He was holding one end of the front transverse pole and walking slowly towards the spot where they would place the horse.

John crouched inside the horse. His feet were on the bottom framework, one on each side of the horse. In his arms he held the equipment. The horse creaked and lurched as the bearers staggered under the unaccustomed weight. They got the horse into position and began to vault.

Inside the horse John worked quickly. Scraping up the dark-grey surface sand, he put it into the cardboard box and started to dig a deep trench for one side of the shoring. He put the bright yellow excavated sand into the trouser-leg bags.

As the trench grew deeper he had difficulty in reaching the bottom. He made it wider and had to bank the extra sand against one end of the horse. It was hot inside the horse and he began to sweat.

He finished the trench and put the plywood sheet in position. He replaced the surface sand, ramming it down with the handle of the trowel, packing the shoring tight. The top of the shoring was six inches below the ground.

Standing on the framework of the horse, he carefully spread the sand over the plywood sheet, packing it down hard, finally sprinkling the grey sand over the whole area covered by the horse – obliterating his foot and finger marks.

Calling softly to Peter, he gave the word that he had finished.

The vaulters inserted the carrying poles and staggered

back into the canteen with John and the bags of sand.

Once inside the canteen they transferred the sand from the trouser-leg bags into long, sausage-like sacks made from the arms and legs of woollen underwear. These they carried away slung round their necks and down inside their trouser legs.

The sand was dispersed in various places around the compound, some of it finding its way by devious routes to the latrines, some of it buried under the huts, some of it carried out in specially made trouser pockets and dug into the tomato patches outside the huts.

It took them four days to sink the four sides of the box. Working alternately, they sank the box in the ground and removed the sand from inside it. When they reached the bottom of the woodwork they dug deeper still, putting bricks under the four corners of the box to support it. They made a trap of bed-boards and replaced this and the surface sand whenever they left the hole.

Finally they had made a hole five feet deep and two feet six inches square. They had dropped the wooden box twelve inches as they worked. The top of the box was now eighteen inches below the surface of the ground. This eighteen inches of sand above the wooden trap gave them security from the probing-rods of the ferrets and was also deep enough to deaden any hollow sound when the trap was walked on. But it was too much sand to remove each time before reaching the trap. To make this easier they filled bags, made from woollen undervests. These they placed on top of the trap, covering them with merely six to eight inches of surface sand. The bags were thin enough not to impede the progress of the ferret's probe, and enabled them to uncover and recover the trap more quickly.

The wooden box stood on four brick piles two feet high. On three sides the shaft below the wooden box was shored with pieces of bed-board. The fourth side was left open for the tunnel.

It was possible to stand in the shaft, but it was not possible to kneel. To get into the tunnel they were forced to make a short burrow in the opposite direction. Into this they thrust their feet while kneeling to enter the tunnel.

The first seven feet of the tunnel was shored solid with bed-boards. The shoring was made by Peter, in the evenings, in the security of their room, and taken down to the tunnel in sections and reassembled there. The whole of the work was done with a table-knife and a red-hot poker. To assemble the shoring Peter lay on his back in the darkness of the narrow tunnel, scraping away sufficient sand to slid the main bearers into position before inserting the bed-boards. He had to work slowly and carefully, fearful all the time that a sudden fall of sand would bury him. He was alone down there and even a small fall of sand would be enough to pin him, helpless, on his back in the narrownesss of the tunnel.

When the ceiling of the tunnel was in position they had to fill the space between the top of the tunnel and the wooden ceiling with sand. If this were not done the sand would fall and the ceiling become higher and higher until a tell-tale subsidence of the surface would reveal the path of the tunnel.

After the first seven feet of shoring, which they built to take the force of the impact of the vaulters on the surface, the tunnel ran on without any shoring whatever.

The tunnel was very small. They had quickly seen that the progress of the work would be determined by the speed with which they could get the excavated sand away. The smaller they made the tunnel the less sand they would have to dispose of and the faster would go the work.

While one of them supervised the vaulting the other dug in the tunnel. He worked alone down there. Once he got into the tunnel with his hands in front of his head he had to stay like that. He could not get his arms behind him again. Nor could he crawl with them doubled up. It was fingers and toes all the way until he got to the end of the tunnel. Once he got there he scraped some sand from the face with the trowel and crawled backwards down the tunnel, dragging the sand with him. When he got back to the vertical shaft he had brought enough sand to fill half a bag. And there were twelve bags to fill.

There was no light in the tunnel and very little air. He worked entirely naked and spent his spell of work in a bath of perspiration. He worked naked because it was cooler and if he wore even the lightest clothes he scraped a certain amount of sand from the sides of the tunnel as he crawled along. Each bag of sand that was scraped from the sides of the tunnel meant one less bag taken from the face. So he worked entirely naked and as he sweated the sand caked on him. When he finished his spell of digging his eyes, ears and nose were full of sand.

They grew segs on their elbows and knees and broke their fingernails. As the tunnel grew longer the work became more difficult and the air more foul. They did not put up air-holes for fear of the dogs.

And so they worked until they had dug a tunnel forty feet long. After forty feet they could do no more. They had reached the limit of their endurance. The farther they pushed the tunnel the more difficult the work became. The air was bad; and they were taking two hours to fill the twelve bags.

Not only were the tunnellers exhausted by the twenty-four times repeated crawl up the tunnel, but the vaulters – who had been vaulting every afternoon of the two months that it had taken to dig the forty feet – were exhausted too. The tunnellers were given extra food, but the vaulters were not, and they had little energy to spare.

57

Peter and John had devised games and variations on the theme of vaulting. A dozen men could not vault for two hours without looking unnatural about it. The whole time one of the tunnellers was below ground the other would be in the vaulting team trying to make the two hours that the horse stood there appear as natural as possible. It was not easy, especially when the ferret was standing within earshot of the horse, watching the vaulting.

They organized a medicine-ball and a deck-tennis quoit and stood in a circle round the horse throwing them to one another. They even organized a run round the circuit – leaving the horse vulnerable and alone with the trap open below it.

It was a considerable physical strain working in the tunnel; yet both of them preferred it to organizing the vaulting.

The end came one afternoon while John was in the tunnel. Peter had gone to the main gate to find out how many Germans were in the compound. It was ten minutes before they were due to take the horse in.

As he was walking back towards the horse he was met by one of the vaulters, pale-faced and running.

'What's wrong?' Peter asked.

'There's been a fall.'

'Where?'

'Near the horse.'

'Is John all right?'

'We shouted to him, but we can't get a reply.'

Peter ran towards the horse. A fall probably meant that John was trapped. There were no air-holes. He would be caught in the end of the tunnel, suffocating, trapped by the fall of sand.

The vaulters were grouped round a man who was lying on the ground. Peter glanced quickly towards the sentry boxes above the wire. The guards were watching.

'Where's the fall?' he asked.

'Wilde's lying on it. A hole suddenly appeared, so Wilde lay on it to stop the guards seeing it. He's pretending he's hurt his leg.'

'How's John?'

'We can't get a reply.'

Peter wanted to overturn the horse at once and go down, but the thought of the discovery of the tunnel stopped him. Old John would be furious if he panicked for nothing.

'Send someone for a stretcher, he said. 'We must make this look as natural as possible.'

Two of the vaulters went for a stretcher. Peter crouched by Nigel's feet, his head near the horse. 'John,' he called. 'John!'

No answer.

'Roll over, Nig,' he said.

Nigel rolled over. There was a hole, about as thick as his arm, going down into the darkness of the tunnel. ' John,' he called. 'John!'

'Hallo, Pete.' The answer was weak.

'What happened?'

'There's been a fall, but I can clear it. I've taken some of the shoring from the shaft. I'll have it fixed in a jiffy. Can you fill it from the top?'

'O.K. Let me know when you've got it fixed.' He pretended to attend to Nigel's leg.

'The goons seem interested,' Nigel said.

'The chaps with the stretcher will be here in a minute,' Peter told him. 'They'll carry you to your hut. That'll explain what we've been doing.'

Presently he heard John's voice, thinly, from inside the tunnel. 'I'm just putting the shoring in. You can fill-in in about five minutes.'

What a man, Peter thought. What a man. Good old John. He poked solicitously at Nigel's leg. The two vaulters returned with the stretcher and a first-aid kit. Peter made a great business of bandaging Nigel's leg while the others, shuffling round, kicked the sand towards the hole.

'It'll sink a bit,' Peter said. 'We'll kick some more over it later on. What's the time?'

'Three-thirty.'

'It's roll-call at four! We must get John up before then.' He banged on the side of the horse. There was no reply.

Ten minutes passed. Still there was no sign from John.

We've had it, Peter thought. If we can't get him up before roll-call we've had it. 'Come on, chaps, let's get vaulting,' he said. 'We can't just stand around here.'

They began to vault again. Then he heard John's voice, urgently, from inside the horse. 'Hey, Pete, what's the time?'

'You've got five minutes.'

'It's an awful mess.'

At the end of the five minutes they carried him into the canteen. He could hardly stand. 'It's an awful mess,' he said. 'There's a bit of tree root there and the vaulting must have shaken it loose. I've jammed it up temporarily but it needs proper shoring.'

'I'll take some down with me tomorrow,' Peter said.

The next afternoon he went down with some wooden shoring. He found the tunnel choked with sand. Soft shifting sand that continued to fall as he worked. He worked in the dark, entirely by feel, and the air was bad so that he panted as he worked. Sand fell into his eyes and his mouth. He worked furiously, clearing the sand away and fitting the shoring into position.

When the shoring was fitted he managed to pack some of the sand away between the shoring and the sides of the tunnel. The rest of it he spread about the floor, lying flat on his belly and pressing it down with his hands.

When he finally got back into the horse he could hardly find the strength to replace the trap. He put it back, and the sand above it, and gave John the signal that he was ready to be taken in. When he reached the canteen he crawled out from under the horse and fainted.

That evening he was taken to the camp hospital. It was a total collapse. He had taken too much out of himself with the digging, the vaulting and the worry. The British doctor prescribed a week in bed. The matter was out of Peter's hands and he lay in bed wondering what John was doing.

During the week he was in the hospital no digging was done; but the horse was taken out every afternoon to avoid the suspicion of the guards.

Chapter Four

Peter Bribes A Guard

Peter had been given a sedative and put to bed. He woke during the night, sweating. Outside it was raining. Outside the window the rain poured down, beating on a corrugated-iron roof somewhere close at hand, drumming and beating and sluicing away into the gutter. Occasionally there was a flash of lightning and a low rumble of thunder in the distance.

He lay in bed and listened to the rain. It sounded cool and soft – summer rain. He imagined it falling on the leaves of a tree outside the window, pattering on the leaves and then falling in large slow drops on to the dark earth below. He imagined it, earth-brown, swirling and gurgling as it made a way for itself down the gravel path; eddying but imperative, with small twigs and leaves like rudderless boats twisting and turning on its surface. Twisting and turning but always following the flow of the stream, underneath the wire, into the ditch outside the wire; the freedom of the outside world.

He lay for a long time listening to the rain and finally fell asleep, cool now, soothed by the patter of the rain.

When he awoke again it was morning. The blackout shutters had been taken from the windows and the sunlight streamed into the room. It seemed more friendly than in the night, and more untidy. The other patients were sitting up in bed, washing themselves. Through the open door he could hear the clanging of buckets and the swish of water as the orderlies washed the floor of the corridor.

He lay still for a while listening to the friendly banter of the other patients. They were ragging the man in the bed next to his own. By his lack of repartee and the sounds coming from his bed it was obvious that he was gargling.

When the gargling was finished he was able to reply. He spoke with a marked Australian accent. 'It was bad luck, that's all. If it hadn't been for that darned sentry we'd have got away.'

Peter raised his head and looked towards the next bed. His neighbour had a bandage round his head and his arm was in a sling.

''Morning, cobber. Feeling better?'

'I've got a lousy head,' Peter said. 'What's wrong with you?'

'I got a bullet through the shoulder. We were just getting a boat at Danzig and a sentry saw us. Took a pot at me and got me through the shoulder. I cut my head open when I fell down.'

62

'He's got a sore throat,' one of the other men said. 'There's nothing wrong with him except the sore throat. He got that talking about his escape. He's done nothing but talk about it since he's been here.'

'He's chocker,' the Australian said. 'Broke his arm jumping off a train. Hadn't been out more than a few hours and he breaks his arm falling off a train. He needs to get some hours in.'

'Where are you from?' Peter asked.

'The North Compound. Four of us got out under the wire. I'd have made it if it hadn't been for that sentry.'

'How long were you out?'

'Three days. I caught this cold sleeping in a ditch.'

'What happened to the other two?'

'In the cooler. Put their hands up as soon as he started shooting. Wish I'd had the sense to do the same.'

'How did you get to Danzig?' Peter asked.

'Jumped a goods train. Riding on the rods, cobber. That's the way for a man to get around.'

'What's Danzig like?'

'Rotten. Wouldn't go there again. No future for a joker there. Too many sentries in the docks.'

'Are the docks fenced in?'

'No, but they're stiff with troops. No future there, cobber.'

That week Peter lay in bed dreaming of escape. He listened carefully to the experiences of the others, comparing them with his own; trying to trace a common weakness in their plans. He thought back over his last attempt, an abortive escape made from Dulag-Luft when he was first captured. That had been over a year ago. A year since then spent in escape, and he had never got within fifty feet of the wire. People said it was impossible to escape, and here were two men who had just been brought back.

He questioned them about their attempt and tried

63

to analyse the causes of its failure. He ran over in his mind all the stories he had heard from prisoners who had been outside the wire. He went over each escape step by step until he came to the moment of capture. In every case they had been caught on foot and usually within a few days of leaving the camp. Most of them had walked, covering sometimes only a very few miles before they were recaptured. Of those who had jumped trains only these two had reached their destination, and they had been caught in the docks in Danzig. They had boarded the train in the goods yard outside the camp and had travelled all the way without a stop.

'That seems to be the answer,' he said one night after lying for some time, pondering, on his bed. 'Buy tickets and travel as passengers. There must be hundreds of foreign workers travelling about Germany on the railway.'

'It's not safe,' the Australian said. 'Bound to get caught first time they ask you for your papers. The things we make aren't good enough to stand a train check.'

'But you are getting somewhere,' Peter persisted. 'If you do get past the booking office you travel quickly and safely to where you want to go.'

'They have train checks,' the Australian said. 'I had a cobber who did that. He got past the booking clerk all right but got picked up on the train. Joker came round looking at the tickets and asking for their papers. When he showed his papers they ran him in straight away. Those jokers are used to looking for forged papers and they spot 'em right away.'

'It must have been a fast train,' Peter said. 'You don't want a corridor train. You want to get on a slow local train, one without a corridor. Once you're in, you're in. Nothing can happen until you get to the other end.'

'Unless you get into conversation with anyone.'

'You can pretend to sleep. Besides, you'd obviously be a foreigner and the Germans wouldn't talk to you anyway.'

'How do you know that they allow foreign workers on the trains? Probably transport 'em in cattle trucks.'

'We'll have to find that out.'

'I'd rather walk,' the Australian said. 'Or jump goods trains. Too nerve-racking to sit in the same carriage with a lot of goons for several hours. Might fall asleep and start talking in English. Besides, they smell. Give me the open air every time.'

'I'm not so sure,' Peter said. 'I think there's something in this train travel.'

After the tension of the last few days it was a relief to lie back and do nothing. It was a queer place, this inner sanctum of captivity. A place remote from barbed wire and goon boxes. The patients were no more prisoners than were the patients in any military hospital. Even the guards were more friendly and, not being supervised, were able to come into the wards and talk to the patients.

Peter used this period of enforced idleness to complete his pictorial record of Kriegie life. He wanted to make a record of the untidiness of boxes and old tin cans in which they lived, the bearded figures wrapped in a multitude of sweaters, scarves and greatcoats, hobbling in their wooden clogs out of the barrack huts to attend the morning appel. The appel itself, rows and rows of ragged figures in balaclava helmets, clad in every type and colour of uniform from French horizon blue through air force blue and English and Polish khaki to the dark blue of the Fleet Air Arm. Every colour of beard from bright red to black, every form of footwear from clogs to flying-boots.

He wanted to paint the hospital, its bare wooden walls and rows of untidy beds. The rough home-made bedside tables, chairs made from packing-cases, and the pale angular patients.

Above all he wanted to capture the spirit of undefeated

humour that was so typical of the camp – the humour that inspired the cartoon that hung on the wall of one of the messes in his block. The drawing showed two Kriegies wrapped up like parcels in scarves and sweaters, trying to heat a tin of food over a fire made from a broken packing-case, the remains of which still lay beside them on the floor. Around them was an indescribable chaos of old tins, bits of wire and sticks or wood, and over all hung the pall of smoke and steam which gathered as soon as the prisoners were locked in for the night. The caption ran, 'Not the Berkeley, old boy – wouldn't be seen dead in the place!'

The first Sunday evening that Peter was in the hospital the camp padre brought a portable gramophone and played a selection of classical records. He played Beethoven's Second Piano Concerto and as Peter lay listening his thoughts travelled back to the night that he had been shot down. The quiet stooging along miles from the target, the moon and the stars, the flickering searchlights far away on the horizon. The lighthearted conversation of his crew. Then suddenly the hammer and din of machine-gun bullets and the heavier tearing impact of cannon shells as a night fighter closed in from behind them. The wild jinking to avoid the attack, the dry-mouthed sick fear of the smashing, tearing impact of the shells. The smell of cordite, the sudden red mushrooming fire in the cockpit, the fumbling with the parachute and the sickening swaying of the flapping parachute as he descended into Germany.

He lived again his feeling of relief to be safely, unhurt, on the ground. The three days hunted across the German countryside, the capture, interrogation, solitary confinement, the prison camp. Improvisation, making the best of things, attempting to escape.

He thought of his first camp, Oflag XXIB in Poland. It had been snowing when the new batch of prisoners had arrived and the night had been clear, smelling of snow and pinewoods. They had been marched into the barrack block where a hundred prisoners had been locked since dusk. After the freshness of the night outside, the stench had been appalling. A long low room lit by dozens of home-made goon lamps, lamps made from tobacco tins filled with rancid animal fat. Lamps which gave off a feeble red glow and clouds of black evil-smelling smoke. They threw weird, distorted shadows on the walls which had once been white-washed but now were grey and smeared by smoke and steam. There were windows in each of the side walls but these were covered from the outside by wooden blackout shutters. The air was thick with tobacco smoke and steam from the row on row of damp washing which hung down almost to head level from lines strung across the room. Smoke from the goon lamps mixed with the steam and tobacco smoke to form a thick fog which eddied and billowed just below the ceiling.

He remembered his horror at the uncouth appearance of the bearded, haggard-looking men who sat huddled round the flickering goon lamps. Life had been pretty grim in those early days. The days before the Red Cross parcels had begun to arrive and the prisoners had lived on turnip soup and rotten potatoes. It seemed almost impossible now, in the heat of the summer, that he had been so cold. He remembered waking in that long damp room, waking fully dressed, even to his issue greatcoat. He wore a woollen skullcap on his head and mittens on his hands. A film of water lay on the grey blanket which covered his head and the woodwork of the bunk on which he lay was damp.

He grinned as he remembered the reveille, the door crashing open and the hoarse baying cry of 'Raus! Raus!' as the guards came into the room. The equally hoarse shout of 'Push off!' with which the prisoners replied. It had been an abrupt introduction to imprisonment, but he had learned a lot at Oflag XXIB.

It had been there that he had met John, the lone army officer among so many airmen. At first he had seemed aloof, but later, when you got to know him, you discovered his eagerness, his consuming desire to escape, to wipe out the disgrace of being captured. It was a disgrace not shared by the airmen because it involved a surrender of arms.

His thoughts were suddenly broken by the clatter of footsteps and the yelping commands of a German officer. The door crashed open and a German major with an escort of soldiers clanked into the ward. They had come to conduct a 'blitz appel.' The major paused, stood looking at the gramophone and its operator, softly illuminated by the flickering yellow glow of a goon lamp. The padre was playing the last movement of the Second Piano Concerto.

'Ach, Beethoven,' the major said. 'He is a good German.'

'Yes,' said the Australian's voice from out of the darkness. 'He's dead!'

The Australian had 'tamed' one of the guards. He called him 'Dopey' and treated him with affectionate contempt. Dopey was a simple man, a man of small loyalties. For a bar of chocolate he would forget his obligation to the Third Reich. For a cigarette he would agree that the Allies would probably win the war.

One day when Dopey came in for his cup of cocoa Peter talked to him about the state of the railways. He began by asking for news of the latest air raids.

'*Hamburg kaput*,' the guard said. '*Duisburg kaput. Haben Sie Zigaretten?*'

Peter gave him a cigarette.

'*Danke.*' He took off his cap. '*Hitler kaput. Deutschland kaput.*'

'Good show, Dopey,' the Australian said. 'How long will the war last?'

'One month, two month.'

'How're the Ruskies doing?' the Australian asked. This stock question always brought the same reply. Dopey was terrified of the Russians.

'Russland no good! Stalingrad no good!' He lifted the leg of his trousers to show where he had been wounded. He had been wounded in the battle of Stalingrad and left lying in the snow. He had been returned to Germany badly frost-bitten, for Home Defence duties. His greatest fear was of being sent back to the Russian front.

'Ruskies good fighters,' the Australian said. 'Ruskies better fighters than Germans.'

'Ruskies no good,' Dopey repeated. 'Ruskies mad devils. Stalingrad no good. Mud. Snow. Ice. Ruski women fight like devils. Not good to fight against women.'

'Not when they're armed,' the Australian said. 'You're not bad at it when they're not.'

'Russland no good,' the guard repeated.

But Peter wanted to get the conversation back to the railways. '*Hamburg Bahnhof kaput?*' he asked.

'*Hamburg kaput.*' The guard knew this by heart. He had been paid a cigarette to say it. He might, with luck, get another. '*Duisburg kaput, Berlin kaput.*'

Peter laughed and tried again. After much questioning he discovered that the railways were overcrowded, trains were running late and, above all, that foreign workers were allowed to travel on the trains. But they had to have special passes. Further indirect questions brought the information that a foreign worker needed permission from the firm by whom he was employed and a special permit from the police before he could leave the town where he was registered.

From that time onward until he left the hospital Peter cultivated Dopey in every way. He gave him cigarettes and cocoa and bribed him with his small ration of chocolate to bring eggs into the hospital. When the time was ripe he asked Dopey to borrow one of the foreign workers' passes and bring it into the camp for him to see.

Dopey refused. He was terrified. Nothing would make him budge. He was willing to trade for small, innocent commodities, but stuck at the passes. It was not patriotism. He was afraid of the consequences.

Peter played his trump card. 'You have been trading with the prisoners. I have three witnesses. If you do not bring me the passes I shall report you to the Camp Kommandant. We shall go to the cooler. But you – you will be shot.'

Dopey whined and pleaded, but he was caught and he knew it. The next morning he brought the passes. Peter made a careful copy of them and returned them to Dopey the same evening. The passes would have to be forged properly when he got back to the camp; but he knew what they were like. He was equipped now and he bided his time. During the long hours of idleness in the hospital he had completed his plans for the journey to neutral territory. He waited impatiently to get back to the tunnel.

Chapter Five

The Third Man

When Peter came out of hospital he and John discussed the tunnel. As usual they discussed it while walking round the circuit, the only place in the compound safe from the ears of the ferrets.

'It's quite obvious,' Peter was saying, 'that we can't go on as we are. We've done forty feet out of the hundred and ten and already we're taking two hours to dig out twelve bags. The farther we get the longer it will take. It looks as though we've come to a full stop.'

'I suppose we couldn't take the horse out twice a day? Once in the morning and once in the afternoon?'

'We could do that but then we could only take six, or at most eight, bags out at a time. And that would grow less and less the farther we got. No, I can't see how we can finish the job under the present system. We've got to think of something altogether new. It's not the digging, it's getting the blasted sand back from the face to the shaft. It's bad enough at forty feet. It's going to be impossible to drag it back the whole length of the tunnel. Why, it'll take about half an hour to crawl up the face once we get to a hundred feet. It's not like wriggling on the surface. It looks as though we've bitten off more than we can chew.'

'There's always a way,' John said. 'Let's study the problem. It's how to get the sand from the face to the shaft. Why not use a toboggan like they did at Schubin?'

'That was a big tunnel and they could have as many down there as they liked. Here we've got no air and no light. Besides, if you took two men out in the horse you couldn't bring any sand back. It would be as much as the vaulters could do to carry the two men, let alone twelve bags of sand as well. And I don't see how a toboggan would help you if you were down there alone.'

'Then we'll *have* to take two down at once, that's all.'

Peter grunted and they walked on in silence. He was still feeling the strangeness of walking on the circuit after the closer confinement of the hospital. We must do it, he thought. It's too good a thing to drop. There must be *some* way of getting the sand out of the place . . .'

Then he saw it. 'I've got an idea,' he said. 'It'll be slow going but I think we'll cope with the whole length of the tunnel.'

'How?'

71

'We'll go down together, as you suggested. We'll have to stand head to head, one at each end of the horse. The chaps should be able to carry us. Then we'll have to make thirty-six bags instead of the original twelve. And we'll have to make a small chamber at the end of the tunnel to give us room to work. We'll run a toboggan between us with a rope at each end. One will work in the chamber and the other in the vertical shaft. We can dig enough in one session to fill the thirty-six bags – it's not the digging that takes the time. When we've filled the thirty-six bags we'll stack them all in the shaft and go back in the horse without any sand.'

'You mean, leave all the thirty-six bags in the tunnel?'

'I'm coming to that. We do that in the afternoon. The same evening one of us goes out alone in the horse and brings back twelve of the bags. The next afternoon the other brings back twelve more, and the last twelve that evening. The next afternoon we both go out and dig another thirty-six.'

'We shan't average more than six inches a day,' John said.

'We'll have to revise our ideas, that's all; and we'll have to bring someone else in to organize the vaulting. We can't both be underground without having someone up there who's in the scheme.'

'I thought just we two were going to be in it. I thought we were going to keep it small.'

'Yes, but we've got to adapt our plans as we go along. It's too much to ask a chap to organize all the vaulting and not give him a chance to go out with us.'

'O.K. Whom do you suggest?'

'Let's ask Tony Winyard. He's done a moling dienst himself and he might help with the digging.'

'O.K. You go and find him and I'll organize some more trouser bottoms and get on with the extra bags.'

Peter found Winyard in the library, looking for a

72

book on old glass. 'Hallo, Tony,' he said. 'Care for a turn round the circuit? There's something I'd like to ask you.'

'Sure – I'm getting bored with glass anyway.' And they walked out into the sunshine of the compound.

'How the dienst going?' Tony spoke casually.

'That's what I wanted to see you about. We need a third man and we wondered if you'd care to join us.'

Winyard did not answer immediately. He seemed slightly embarrassed. 'Well, as a matter of fact, I'm just preparing for a dienst myself. It's a one-man show – under the wire in the Vorlager – but it won't come off until the autumn. I've got to wait for the dark evenings.'

'Oh, we shall be out before the autumn,' Peter said. 'We're just starting a new system. We hope to get cracking again at once.'

Winyard appeared to be thinking it over. 'I'd like to,' he said finally, 'but I'll have to turn it down, I'm afraid. You see I've been caught so often that they've told me that next time I'm caught I'm for the Straflager and once you get there you're finished. My next attempt has got to be pretty nearly a dead certainty. Not that yours isn't a good show,' he added quickly, 'but frankly I don't think you stand much chance of getting out.'

'O.K.,' Peter said. 'I can see your point.'

'Don't think I'm knocking your show in any way,' he repeated. 'There's nothing wrong with the idea except that it's going to take so long. I'm afraid the goons are bound to tumble to it before you're finished.'

'Oh, I don't think so. We've got over the worst part. The horse has been accepted as a camp institution now. The goons are used to it and think no more about it.'

'How much have you done now?'

'About forty feet.'

'How much have you got to do in all?'

'A hundred and ten.'

'And you've been at it how long – two months?'

'Yes.'

'It's the end of August now – that puts you well into November.'

'No, I reckon October. We'll mole the last ten or fifteen feet and do it in one go.'

'Oh, well, I wish you luck. I've had moling, but if you want any tips I'll be glad to tell you all I can.'

'Thanks a lot,' Peter said. 'I shall be glad of that. We've never tried a moling dienst before.'

He found John at the far end of the camp canvassing for trouser-leg bottoms. 'How's it going, John?'

'Oh, I've exhausted all the people who've cut their trousers down. I'm now persuading people that shorts are a good thing and getting 'em to cut 'em down while I wait.'

'Winyard doesn't want to come in with us,' Peter said. 'He doesn't think we've an earthly chance of getting out.'

'That's his funeral. I've got enough bottoms for another ten bags.'

'Who do we ask now?' Peter said. 'I'd like to ask old Nig, but his leg's so dicky I don't think he'd make it.'

'We shouldn't have let him do so much vaulting. With a wounded leg like his it was asking for trouble. He can hardly walk now and yet he comes out every day and hops round the horse – just to make it look a crowd. He ought to go into hospital.'

'What's wrong with his leg exactly?'

'Oh, it was badly patched up by a goon doctor. They shot at him while he was coming down in a parachute.'

'How do you know they shot *at* him? I expect they were just popping off wildly at everything in general.'

74

'Why do you always stand up for the Hun, Pete? You must have lost more than most people in the war.'

'Oh, I don't know. It wasn't anyone's fault. You can't go blaming the whole nation. Nig doesn't blame them for his leg.'

'Old Phil blames them – makes goon hatred a sort of religion. He gets up every morning cursing the goons and keeps it up all day.'

'I suppose some chaps work up a hate to keep them going – a useful way of expending surplus energy.'

'He's helped us a lot,' John said. 'He's organized practically all the dispersal, as well as vaulting with the best of them.'

'He's not much good at vaulting.'

John smiled. 'I love to see him when he gets really angry. He grits his teeth and charges at the horse with his arms going like piston-rods.'

'But the nearer he gets to the horse the slower he runs.'

'Yes, but he does keep at it. He's improved enormously since he started.'

'Let's ask him to come in,' Peter said. 'We'll do the digging and he can organize the vaulting and the dispersal. I'd rather no one else went down the hole because we know exactly how small we want it, and Phil would have grand ideas about enlarging it and putting in an air pump. If he'd look after the vaulting – you know how methodical he is, he'd draw up lists and organize it so that everyone had a certain time on a certain day to vault. Now that we're going to go out twice a day the problem of the vaulters is going to be more difficult than ever.'

'O.K.,' John said, 'let's go and find him.'

They ran Philip Rowe to earth near the gate leading to the Vorlager. He had a list of names in his hand and was looking worried.

'What's the gen, Phil?' asked Peter. 'Come for a turn round the circuit.'

'I can't at the moment. I'm supposed to be organizing the hot showers. But no one seems to want one.'

'Then leave it,' Peter said. 'Come for a walk instead.'

'I can't. It's all right for you – you've no sense of responsibility. I've got a job to do. Someone's got to help run the camp.'

'Come on, Phil,' John said. They fell in one each side of him and began to walk him firmly round the circuit.

'All right,' he said, accepting the inevitable. 'But only once round. I've got to find these people for their showers.'

'We've more important things than showers,' Peter said. 'We're going to get you out of the camp and send you home to your wife.'

'You're mad,' Philip said. 'You're both mad. Let me go – find someone else to pester. I've got a job to do.'

'We mean it, Phil,' John said. 'We want you to join us in the dienst.'

Philip looked suspicious. 'Why ask me?'

'Well,' Peter began, 'knowing your organizing abil-ity . . .'

'And your almost touching faith in our efficiency . . .' John continued.

'We thought you'd jump at the idea,' Peter concluded.

'What do you want me to do?'

'We're going to work on a new system now. We're both going down together – with a toboggan and rope – and we'll dig thirty-six bags in one session and then spend the next three sessions taking twelve out at a time. We'd like you to organize the vaulting and the dispersal of the sand.'

'I'm practically doing that already.'

'That's why we want you to come in. We can get three out as easily as two.'

'O.K.,' Philip said. 'I'll come in. But I don't think we've a hope in hell of ever getting out.'

'You stick by us,' John assured him. 'You'll get out.'

In Peter's mess there was a growing air of tension. They had been at Sagan now for five months, and five months' intimate knowledge of one another was becoming unbearable.

It was lunchtime. The biscuits had not been buttered. No one had gone for the tea water. Five morose figures sat round a bare table. Presently Pomfret spoke. 'It's a matter of principle. I've done it every day this week and now it's Friday. It's not that I mind doing it, but I've done more than my share. Clinton must do it today as a matter of principle.' He advanced his chin obstinately. He was dressed in the full uniform of a flight-lieutenant. His collar, ironed with a tin of hot water, was frayed round the edges.

'That's all very well,' Bennett pointed out, 'but it's lunchtime and we're hungry. You and Clinton share the duty of cook and it's up to you to see that the meal is prepared.' Apart from his odd assortment of clothing Bennett might have been addressing a board meeting. He delivered his opinion as an ultimatum and glanced round the table for approval. His red, hairy arms were crossed upon the table. Having delivered his speech, he sucked his teeth with an air of finality.

'Well, I'm not doing it,' Pomfret said. He appeared about to cry. 'It's not fair! Just because he's digging a tunnel it doesn't mean he can neglect all his duties in the mess. I'm fed up with doing two people's work. All they think about is their wretched tunnel. I'm sick to death of seeing them sitting in the corner whispering all evening. It was bad enough before they started the tunnel. Clinton was always missing at meal times. But for the last two months I've done all the work. It's not right, you know.'

'That's for you and Clinton to settle between yourselves,' said Bennett judicially. 'What about our lunch?

It's only a matter of buttering eight biscuits and walking over to the canteen for some hot water.'

'That's not the point! It's a matter of principle!'

'So the whole mess must suffer for the sake of your principles,' put in Robbie, who was sitting at the head of the table disgustedly studying his fingernails.

'It's not my principles at fault, it's Clinton's laziness.'

'I don't call it laziness to dig in a tunnel and vault over a horse for several hours a day,' Robbie said. 'Surely you and he can come to some arrangement so that you both do an equal amount of work, but his share doesn't interfere with his tunnelling.'

'You can't come to any arrangement with Clinton,' Pomfret said. 'He always forgets. He hasn't grown up yet. He's got no sense of responsibility.'

'He's not the only one who hasn't grown up,' Robbie said.

'This is all very well,' Bennett interrupted, 'but do we get our lunch?'

'I'm not doing it!' said Pomfret obstinately.

The five men looked at one another angrily. The food cupboard was sacred. No one but the cook was allowed to open it. It was a custom of the mess. In a life where hunger was ubiquitous, food had strict taboos.

'Supposing we split the mess in two,' Pomfret said. 'Let them mess together and we five will mess together. They can do what they like then.'

'They always do.' Bennett sucked his teeth.

'Well, what do you say?' Pomfret asked. 'I think it would serve them right.'

'Very likely buck them no end,' Robbie said.

'I think we ought to,' Pomfret said. 'Howard and Clinton can't cook anyway.'

They hesitated. It was a decision. Some of them had not made a decision for years. Some were reluctant to cast the three into the outer darkness of their dissociation.

'I think we should,' Pomfret said.

'Let's take a vote.' Bennett was once more addressing the board of directors.

'I say yes,' Pomfret said.

Bennett looked at Robbie, who thought of coping with the eccentricities of the other three. He decided not to risk it. Anyway, their tunnel would be finished soon.

'I think it's childish,' he said, 'and it'll be damned inconvenient having two messes in one room.'

'Would you rather go with them? Then you can do all the cooking for them,' said Pomfret spitefully.

'No, I'll go with you. But I don't like the idea of splitting up.'

When the others came in they found the biscuits ready buttered and the tea water in the can. John had been working at the face and Peter at the tunnel entrance. Nigel had been hiding the excavated sand under the floor of the canteen. John, yellow from head to foot with caked sweat and sand, threw himself on his bunk and closed his eyes.

'Lunch, John?' Peter asked.

'Not for the moment, thanks, old boy.'

'Feeling rotten?'

'I'm O.K. I'll be O.K. in a minute. I'll wash before I eat.' He lay back with his eyes closed. His body was brown but his face was colourless. His hair, matted with sand and sweat, was damp on his forehead. There were long streams down his chest and arms where the sweat had washed away the sand. The sand was under his broken fingernails and in his eyes. As he lay there, Peter could see that his nostrils too were filled with sand.

Pomfret cleared his throat. 'I prepared the lunch to-day.'

'Thanks, old boy,' John said. 'Was it my turn?'

'It was your turn,' Pomfret replied. 'It has been your

79

turn for the last three days. As a matter of principle I, at first, refused to do it today.'

'Thanks for doing it all the same,' John said. 'I'll do the dinner.'

'That will not be necessary,' Pomfret said. 'We five have decided to mess separately.'

'After due consideration,' said Bennett, addressing an audience of at least five hundred, 'we have decided that we five shall mess on our own.'

Pomfret looked at him angrily. After all, he was in the chair.

'We are tired of Clinton's impossible attitude,' Bennett continued, 'and we presumed that you three would want to be together. We have separated the food, and starting with dinner tonight we shall cater for ourselves.'

'O.K.,' Peter said. 'That suits us.' In a way he was glad as very soon they would begin to save their food for the escape. 'What do you say, Nig?'

'*Blond genug*, old boy,' Nigel replied.

So the mess was split into two and settled down to a new way of living. There was still friction among the five, particularly between Robbie and Bennett, but the three drifted into an ideal way of living where no one was stooge and yet at the right time, for them, the meals appeared. Most of their time was spent in vaulting and digging, making civilian clothes and tracing maps. When they had nothing to do they lay in the sun. They had dug a sand pit outside the window of the mess and, despite spirited opposition from the 'purity league' led by Pomfret, used to lie for hours soaking in the sun that beat back in a shimmering haze from the burning sand. They bathed in a brick fire-water tank and made fantastic sun-hats from Red Cross boxes. But Pomfret hated the sun. He would lie on his bunk cursing the heat, flapping at the flies that buzzed and whined around his head.

The place was thick with flies. Sometimes Peter, John

and Nigel would organize a 'daylight sweep.' They closed the doors and windows and attacked the flies with tightly rolled copies of the *Völkischer Beobachter*, slashing and cutting at the enemy as he settled on table, stools and bunks. It was glorious while it lasted. A slaughter that relieved the tension of their nerves. Finally, flushed and elated with their victory, they would all descend on the sole remaining insect, upsetting stools and tables in their mad rush to claim the last of the intruders. Having cleared the room, they would go and swim in the fire-water tank, returning to find the room as thick with flies as ever.

Peter made a refrigerator consisting of an open-sided wooden cupboard standing on two bricks in a shallow metal tray of water. A loose cover made from a blanket was fitted over the cupboard, its ends falling into the water in the tray. Another metal tray of water was placed on top of the cupboard and 'feeders' – narrow strips of blanket – were led from the upper tray on to the loose cover. By keeping both tins full of water the absorbent loose cover was always moist and the constant evaporation of this moisture considerably lowered the temperature inside the cupboard. So effective was the refrigerator that tins of food placed inside it soon became coated with beads of moisture.

They filled a canvas kitbag with water and hung it from the ceiling of the room. Water oozing through the canvas and evaporating cooled the atmosphere that otherwise would have been unbearable. The sun blazed down on the wooden huts and turned them into ovens. At intervals German soldiers came round with hoses and sprayed water both on the roofs and under the huts.

In the evenings after dinner the prisoners would sit on the steps of their huts or stand in groups against the wooden walls engaged in desultory conversation. It reminded Peter of the slums in Liverpool where he had lived before the war. He had often pitied the people in those slums, sitting in rows on their doorsteps and on chairs on the pavement outside their houses, too hot to go inside their overcrowded tenements. Now he, too, sat in shirt sleeves, smoking his pipe on the doorstep, the dust of the circuit between his toes and the friendly gossip of his neighbours all around him. And sitting there he would feel a quiet contentment, a lazy acceptance of conditions. An acceptance that he knew was dangerous and which he banished with redoubled efforts to escape.

Chapter Six

They Plan Their Journey

It was evening and they had been locked in for the night. Peter and John sat on one of the bunks sewing the trouser-leg bags. It was unbearably hot in the small room. While the lights were on the prisoners were not allowed to remove the wooden blackout shutters, and the air was stale and thick with tobacco smoke. Outside in the corridor the duty stooge sat reading a book.

In other rooms along the corridor other prisoners were making parts of a secret wireless set, forging passports or making civilian clothing from odd bits of uniform. Through the thin partition wall on one side could be heard the strains of a well-worn jazz record. From the other side came the raised voices of two of the prisoners who were quarrelling.

Robbie, Bennett, David and Paul were playing bridge. Pomfret, an angry expression on his face, was trying to read a book.

Nigel was making a golf ball. He had searched for

several days in the compound before he had found the right stone. Smooth, round and not too heavy, it was an ideal stone for the core. Next he had unravelled the top of a pair of woollen socks, carefully winding the wool on to a piece of stick. It was good, resilient wool, resilient enough to give the ball sufficient 'life' to enable him to drive it fifty or sixty yards. He had cut down a pair of issue boots to make shoes and saved the soft leather of the uppers to make the cover of the ball. He had borrowed a paper template and cut two pieces of leather shaped like a solid figure eight. After winding the wool on to the stone until the ball had reached the regulation size, he had soaked the leather in water and was now sewing it together with thread waterproofed with candle grease. Sitting on his bunk, tongue between his teeth, he was gently stretching the damp leather round the ball.

Through the thin partition came the sound of next door's worn-out gramophone.

'That's the end,' Pomfret said. 'That's the end of reading for tonight.'

'Bet you what you like the next tune's "Boynk Boynk",' Nigel said.

'Right,' said Peter. 'I'll take you on. Twenty Player's it's "Ah, Sweet Mystery of Life".'

'I'm in this,' John said. 'Bet it's "Intermezzo".'

Patiently they waited for the record to begin.

'There you are,' Nigel said. 'It's "Boynk Boynk".'

'It isn't "Boynk Boynk" anyway,' Pomfret said, 'it's "Oynk Oynk".'

'It's not,' Nigel said, 'it's "Boynk Boynk".'

'It's "Oynk Oynk" I tell you!' Pomfret said. 'Listen!'

'Oh dear! Are you two arguing again?' John said.

Reedily the stupid tune ground its way into the chorus. 'Oynk Oynk Boogie Boogie Woogie.'

'It's "Boynk"!' Nigel said.

'It's "Oynk"!' Pomfret said.

There was a knock on the door and Stafford, the hut representative on the Escape Committee, brought in a Red Cross box filled with invalid food – the special diet sent from England for the hospital. A certain amount of this food usually found its way into the hands of the Committee and was rationed out to prisoners who were working in tunnels.

Peter made a place for him among the trouser-leg bags on the bed.

'I've got the extra rations,' Stafford said.

'Thanks,' Peter said. 'Any news of the torch?'

'Yes – we'll have it tomorrow. We've only two batteries so you'll have to use it as sparingly as you can.'

'How did you manage it?' John asked.

'Oh, we've got one of the goons taped. Why are you making so many bags?'

They told him of the new system.

'We thought you'd have to do that in the end,' Stafford said. 'Far too much for one man to do. Have you decided on your route and what you're going as?'

'We thought we'd go up to the Baltic and try to stow away on a Swedish boat,' Peter said.

'How are you travelling? As Poles?'

'No,' John said. 'Good-class French workers. Not ex-P.O.W.s, but French craftsmen who've been brought over from France. My French is fairly good. Lived in France some time before the war. And we're both dark enough to pass as Frenchmen.'

'Can you let us have any money?' Peter asked.

'We've got a bit in the kitty – what about two hundred marks apiece?'

'Like a bit more than that if you can manage it. Y'see, we thought we'd travel first class and stay at decent hotels if necessary.'

Stafford looked surprised. 'I say – that's going it a bit,

isn't it? Don't you think that's rather sticking your necks out?'

'No,' John said. 'We've thought it over pretty carefully. Most chaps who've tried to escape have gone out looking like tramps. They may have been out some time but they haven't got very far. If you travel by passenger train it's all or nothing. You're either where you want to be in a few days – or you're caught. We don't think anyone has stayed in a hotel yet, so we thought we'd try it.'

'Perhaps you're right – anyway, it's your show. We'll let you have the money and fix you up with papers and everything you want. If you make it you'll be the first out for over a year.'

'Thanks a lot, Stafford,' Peter said. 'What about a spot of vaulting tomorrow?'

Stafford grinned. 'Opportunist, aren't you? O.K., I'll come and vault. Call in at my room as you go out.'

'Right,' Peter said.

'Oh, by the way,' Stafford added, 'they're starting a tunnel from Block 64. Shouldn't interfere with yours in any way. It's an old one that was sealed up some time ago and Odell is getting it going again. It'll be a blitz job – they'll work continually, in shifts, and stuff all the sand in the roof of their hut.'

'But that's silly,' Peter said. 'The goons search the roof once a week.'

'That's just the idea. They'll wait until the next search and start immediately afterwards. They won't hide the sand at all – just bung it up in the roof – and by working in shifts all day and all night they hope to get out by the next time the roof is searched.'

'How far have they got to go?' Peter asked.

'About a hundred and fifty feet.'

'They won't get all that in the roof. The whole hut'll collapse with all that weight.'

'They'll just put all they can in the roof and then the

last few days they'll put it in their beds and in Red Cross boxes under the beds.'

'How many are going out?'

'The whole hut.'

'They won't have a chance.' Peter was getting angry now. The quick, prison camp anger that fades as quickly as it comes. 'That's about a hundred men. If a hundred men get out now they'll have a country-wide search and then where will *we* be? They won't have all the papers – or the proper clothing. And there'll be such a flap that it'll completely spoil our show.'

'Oh, it's not as bad as that,' Stafford said. 'The whole thing will be over inside a fortnight and it will be at least two months before yours breaks. The flap'll be over by then. Personally, I don't think they'll last more than a few days. But it's an attempt and they're so few and far between these days that we back anything that's put forward.' He grinned. 'Otherwise, you wouldn't have stood much chance.'

'They'll be picked up by the seismographs,' John said.

'Yes, particularly if they work at that speed,' Peter agreed. He was feeling better now.

'It's a wonder you haven't been picked up,' Stafford said.

Peter laughed. 'Ours isn't such a dim scheme as you imagine. Anything picked up by the seismographs is blanketed by the vibration of the vaulters landing on the surface.'

'I hadn't thought of that!' Stafford said.

'No, nor did we until the tunnel had been going for some time,' John admitted. 'Must have been that. The seismographs would have recorded it otherwise.'

'Oh, well,' Stafford yawned. 'I've got to relieve the stooge.' He stood up and stretched. 'Don't forget to call for me tomorrow.'

'We won't forget,' John said.

When he had gone Peter turned to John. 'It's a good thing about Odell, really. I think the goons are getting a bit suspicious and if they find any of our sand they'll blame it on Odell. Now, what about that sketch?' He crossed to his locker and came back with a half-finished sketch of John.

Pomfret sat at the head of the table deeply immersed in his book. Pomfret hated women novelists. In his opinion, everything written by a woman was bad. Pomfret had very fixed ideas about a woman's duties and writing books was not one of them. One of his favourite forms of self-torture was to take a book by one of the more popular women novelists and read it slowly word by word, suffering as much as he could in the process. This evening he was enjoying himself. Sitting, head in hands, he tried to deafen himself to the bridge post-mortem that was raging at the end of the table. He looked up.

'Pete,' he said, 'what's a solid bar of misery?'

'What, old boy?'

'A solid bar of misery.'

Peter was busy with an india rubber.

'What's that, old boy?'

'That's what I want to know. It says here "a solid bar of misery seized her by the throat." Now, what's a solid bar of misery? Just imagine' – he made a gesture with his hands indicating a bar – 'a solid bar' – he illustrated it on the table – 'seized her by the throat.' He seized his throat with both hands and nearly throttled himself. 'I don't get it, do you?'

'No,' Peter said, 'I don't. Hey, Nig, what's a solid bar of misery?'

Nigel thought for a moment. 'A crowded pub that's run out of beer, I should think.'

'What about a brew?' John asked.

'Good show,' said Bennett. 'Our jug's on the fire now. It was pretty hot when I went down there ten minutes ago.'

Although the mess had split in two they still shared the tea, coffee and cocoa. It was more economical.

'I'll do it,' Robbie offered. 'I've finished my book.' He took down the eight mugs and put them on the table.

'Which shall it be,' he asked, 'cocoa, or Nescafé?'

'There's not much Nescafé left,' said Paul, who was cook.

'O.K.,' Robbie said, 'cocoa.' He put the cocoa in the mugs and went down the corridor, returning with the jug of hot water. 'Someone's got a lovely cake in the oven,' he said.

'It's mess three,' Paul told him. 'It's Smith's birthday.'

'Well, that's that!' Peter said, laying down the drawing. 'It's not much like you, I'm afraid, John. But that's about all I can do to it.' He leaned the drawing against the table and stood back. It was a full-length study in pencil and charcoal. It lacked finish but it had caught something of the character of the sitter. It showed a young man in a creased, collarless, woollen shirt, sitting with a book in his lap, his back propped against one of the wooden uprights of the bunk. His right leg was crossed over his left knee. A wooden-soled sandal hung from his right foot, secured by strips cut from an R.A.F. greatcoat. The face was in repose. Dark-skinned, with large brown eyes and heavily marked eyebrows, it was at once sensitive and mischievous. There was something faun-like in the setting of the ears and the long black hair. The subject looked as though he were about to speak. He looked as though what he was about to say would be of interest.

'It's not good,' Peter said, 'but it's the best I've done. Sorry I kept you sitting so long.'

'That's O.K. What about a game of chess?'

'Right.' He knocked out his pipe on the stove and filled it from a tin on the table. He lit it with a cigarette end and a piece of paper. 'If you ever see anyone do this after the war,' he said, 'you'll know he's been a Kriegie.'

'You won't see anyone do it,' John said. 'There'll be plenty of matches.'

'"The listening horizon,"' Pomfret quoted. 'How can a horizon listen?'

'That's poetic licence,' Bennett told him. 'She means it was quiet.'

'Then why doesn't she say "it was quiet"?' Pomfret asked plaintively. '"She raised her eyes to the listening horizon" – it's nonsense.'

'It gives you a lot of pleasure anyway,' Robbie said.

'If I start anything I like to finish it,' Pomfret said. 'I started the book and I'm going to finish it.' He scowled and returned to his torture. Pomfret was enjoying his evening.

John fetched the chess set from a shelf over his bed and put it on a corner of the table. He set out the men. 'I'll give you a knight, if you like, Pete.'

'It would make a better game,' Peter agreed. He sat cross-legged on the bench, puffing at his pipe. He was not a good chess player but he enjoyed the game. He had never beaten John.

The bridge four had broken up and the players were preparing for bed. Bennett was washing his feet in a bowl of water near the stove.

'Have you heard about the new chap in room ten?' Bennett asked.

'What chap?' Nigel said.

'The chap they call "Harry the Horse"?'

'Oh, you mean "Gilbert the Gelding" – the type who's just had his head shaved.'

'Yes, he's an incredible type. Too good-natured to be true. The chaps in room ten have been pulling his leg left, right and centre.'

'I heard about it,' Robbie said. 'It's a darn' shame.'

'What did they do?' Nigel asked.

'They were all sitting in their room one night,' said

Bennett, 'when a chap came in and said, "Have you heard the new order from the S.B.O.?" "No," they said, "what's that?" "Oh," says the first type, "the S.B.O. says we've all got to have our heads shaved as a demonstration against the Hun." Well, they argued who was to be done first and then someone said, "Harry's the newest arrival, let's do him first." So they sat him in a chair and got a razor and soap and shaved his hair off. He had a terrific mop too. Just as they'd finished another type came in and said, "You know about the order to shave our heads – well, it's been cancelled!"'

When the laughter died down Bennett continued, 'The next day they told him they were digging a tunnel from underneath the room and explained that they wanted a lot of water to wash the sand. They collected some buckets and kept Harry staggering between the washhouse and room ten with buckets of water all afternoon. As fast as he brought a full bucket they handed him an empty one and tipped the full one out of the opposite window. Kept it up for about two hours.'

'I think it's a shame,' Robbie said.

'Oh, he doesn't mind – he likes it. You know that skeleton old Mac got from Berlin for his medical studies? They dressed that up one night and sat it up in a chair. When Harry came in he got the fright of his life. "What's that?" he asked. "That's old Joe," they said. "He was one of the earliest Kriegies – died years ago and we're still drawing his rations."'

'It's quite true,' Nigel said, 'and he doesn't turn a hair. I was in room ten the other night. We were all sitting talking and Harry was reading a book. Presently the door opened and a chap dressed in full uniform came in on all fours. No one except Harry took any notice. This type crawled solemnly round the room four times, then stopped in front of Harry and barked, "Stand up when I talk to you! Don't you know I'm your C.O.?" Then

90

he crawled out. One of the chaps closed the door after him and said to Harry, "Don't mind him – he's round the bend."'

The lights flickered twice. 'Lights out in five minutes,' Bennett said. 'You types had better get to bed.'

'O.K.,' Peter said. 'I can't win anyway. Your game, John.'

'Yes, I think so,' John said.

They undressed and Peter put out the light. He crossed to the window and opened the blackout shutters. The night air was clean and cool after the atmosphere of the room. The compound was flooded with moonlight. The sand was silver and the posts of the wire fence stood out straight and dark and edged with light. The top of the sentry box was silver too. Even the yellow searchlights semed powerless against the silver of the moon.

'The goon's in his box and all's well with the world,' he said.

'I hope he falls out of it,' said Robbie.

Chapter Seven

The Tunnel Is In Danger

The camp barber was clipping the hair of a newly-arrived prisoner. On chairs arranged along the wall sat other clients looking at German magazines and waiting their turn to be clipped. Near the window stood a tall, gangling prisoner with a shaven head and long sensitive face. He held a violin under his chin and played a low, sad melody, rising and falling and endlessly repeating the same few notes. He gazed out of the window seemingly unconscious of the other people in the room. Except for the low notes of the violin, the sound of a blue-bottle buzzing against the window-pane and the snip-snap of the barber's scissors, the room was silent.

It was nearly tea time. Outside in the compound a football match was noisily coming to an end; the vaulters were packing up and before long the circuit would be deserted while the prisoners ate their tea.

The newly-arrived prisoner – this was his first visit to the barber's shop – was presently astounded to see the door open and a naked, brown tousle-headed, sand- and sweat-stained figure crawl in on all fours carrying with him a khaki-coloured bag tied at the neck with string.

Without saying a word, ignored by the barber and his waiting clients, the strange figure crawled to the window, opened a trap in the floor and disappeared from view, dragging after him the bag tied with string. Then another fully-dressed figure appeared with another bag, followed by others who formed a human chain, passing the bags from hand to hand down to the naked one under the floor.

Suddenly the vacant-eyed violinist stopped playing. The trap was at once closed on the man under the floor and the human chain became an orchestra earnestly playing the various instruments which had been lying close to hand.

A few minutes later one of the ferrets sauntered past the window. He did not look in. He would have seen only a prisoner having his hair cut, the waiting clients and the camp orchestra practising in one corner of the room. The orchestra continued to play. There was a loud knock on the door. They laid down their instruments and opened the trap. The violinist resumed his melancholy tune. Twelve empty bags were handed up from the hole in the floor and the naked one emerged, carefully dusting the moist sand from his body on to the floor near the trap. He was handed his clothes in silence and in silence

92

he put them on. The sand was brushed into the hole in the floor and the trap carefully replaced. The empty bags were collected while one of the vaulters carefully swept the floor with his handkerchief to remove the last traces of the sand.

After some months of work in the tunnel the space below the floor of the barber's shop was filled. The bags of sand were then carried out by the camp glee-singers, who rehearsed in the next room. The full bags were passed up through a trap door in the ceiling to Nigel, who spread the sand evenly between the joists in the beaverboard ceiling. They could not put much sand in the roof as the weight threatened to bring down the ceiling; so after a time another trap door was made over the kitchen. The bags were now handed up to Nigel, who carried them, bag by bag, across the rafters to the new trap door, where he hid them until the late evening.

Next door to the kitchen was the office of the 'kitchen goon' – the German soldier who supervised the issue of the prisoners' rations. After the kitchen goon had left for the night the bags were handed down into the kitchen, where David was waiting to receive them. When the bags had all been passed down into the kitchen they were carried through to the kitchen goon's office where they were taken down through another trap door and the sand hidden under the floor.

During the daytime the kitchen goon sat in his office completely unaware of the previous evening's work lying directly beneath his feet.

The week that Odell's tunnel was started the Germans pounced again. Peter and John had been digging in the tunnel that afternoon and Peter had been out in the early evening to bring in twelve of the bags. After helping to pass the bags up to Nigel in the roof he had washed himself in the kitchen and was walking back to the hut when he saw the compound gates open and a German army lorry drive at full speed towards the canteen.

He knew at once what was about to happen and he could do nothing to stop it. The lorry would be outside the canteen before the stooges were aware that anything was wrong. The dispersal team was in the roof and under the floor. It was finished. All those months of work would be wasted. All their carefully laid shoring, the brick piles and the cunningly made trap would be exposed, lying on the surface, a pitiful heap of boards and sheets of rotted plywood. He felt sick and walked blindly on round the circuit, his hands in his pockets, walking hard to fight down the sickness and the choking obstruction in his throat. Someone passed him on the circuit and said something about 'Bad luck.' But he did not reply. They had been digging for three months and now the tunnel would be discovered. Three months of pinning your faith to a hole in the ground. Three months of waking up in the morning just a little happier because you were doing something to get out of the place. Three months of jealous anxiety that the hole would be discovered; subterfuge and improvisation, hilarity and panic. Every inch of the narrow hole that had been scraped with their bare hands and a bricklayer's trowel. And now it was all going for nothing.

He would recover. In half an hour he would be grinning and saying, 'It was a lousy tunnel anyway'; but for the moment he was very near to tears and he wanted to be alone.

Soon he was joined by John and they walked on in silence. Peter spoke first. 'Have they caught Nig and the others?' He was deliberately casual.

'No. If you remember we started an hour earlier today. David was just climbing out of the kitchen window as the goons rushed in at the door. He was the last one out.'

'Where did Nig go?'

'He climbed down into the canteen and joined the glee-singers. When the goons rushed in they were singing "He shall set His angels guard over thee." The Feldwebel stood under the trap while they sent a ferret up from the kitchen side. All they got out was the ferret.'

'They'll find the sand in the roof,' Peter said.

'I'm afraid they will. They turned the singers out but Nig stayed behind as long as he could collecting the sheets of music. When he left they were tearing up the floor of the barber's shop.'

'I'm afraid we've had it.'

'There's still a chance. They may not connect the horse with it. They may think we were dispersing the sand from somewhere else. Or if they do think of the horse they may think it was part of the stooging system.'

'Were there any bags left in the kitchen?'

'Yes – they'd all finished except Nig and David who were stowing the stuff away under the office floor. When the alarm went they still had three full bags, so they stuffed the three full ones and all the empty ones down the trap, closed it up, and David went out of the window and Nig went up through the trap, over the roof and down into the canteen.'

'That was jolly good work.'

John laughed. 'It was Nig and David. They'd rather go to the cooler than leave a trap open. If the ferrets don't discover the trap under the office all they'll find will be a lot of sand and nothing to tell them where it came from.'

'If they do find the bags we're finished,' Peter said. 'They're much too big for the goons to think we carried them under our coats. If they do find them they'll know the tunnel's somewhere in the canteen and when they can't find it they'll either watch the place so closely that we can't work or they'll connect them with the horse. If only we could lay a false trail away from the canteen we might stand a chance.'

'Let's walk round there,' John suggested, 'and have a look.'

There was an armed guard posted outside the canteen. From inside came the sounds of hammering and the hoarse commands of the German N.C.O.

'They're enjoying themselves,' John said gloomily. 'They're tearing the place to pieces.'

Peter did not speak.

'This puts paid to Odell's scheme,' John said. 'The ferrets will ransack the camp looking for the tunnel and more dispersal. They're bound to examine all the roofs – especially after they found our sand in the canteen roof.'

'Have you got the rest of the bags?' Peter asked quickly.

'There are twenty-four full ones in the tunnel and a few odds and ends in my bed.'

'Let's go and get them,' Peter said, 'and bung them in with Odell's sand. If it's not discovered it will be O.K.; and if it *is* discovered it won't do Odell any harm. But it'll make the goons think our dispersal was part of Odell's tunnel. I don't think trouser-leg bags have been used before and they're bound to put two and two together and think Odell's men got them across in some way or other from their hut to the canteen. If we can persuade them that the canteen sand came from Odell's tunnel we can lie low for about a week and then go on using the canteen for dispersal. They won't search there again for a bit once they think they know where the sand came from.'

'Right,' John said. 'You go and tell Odell and I'll get the bags and meet you in his room.'

The next morning when the prisoners went out to appel they took with them enough food to last them all day. They knew the camp would be searched and during

96

the evening they had hidden most of their *verboten* possessions behind the panelling of the walls and in the sand under the huts. Some of them, risking the possibility of a personal search, carried their most cherished possessions with them.

During the day Odell's tunnel was discovered. It was discovered by the ceiling of Hut 64 collapsing and burying the searchers in a shower of sand. They soon found the tunnel and with it the bags that Peter had hidden there the night before. Apparently satisfied that this was the only tunnel in existence, they called off the search and took the senior officer of the hut to serve his sentence in the cooler.

That night, after they had been locked in the huts, Stafford came in to cheer them up. He brought with him the weekly ration of milk food.

'They've found the trap in the floor of the kitchen goon's office,' he said. 'Marcus was over there getting water just before lock-up time.'

'That means they've found the bags,' Peter said.

'What are you going to do?'

'Nothing,' Peter said. 'Nothing for a week – or perhaps more. We shall take the horse out every day and vault as usual. But no digging. No digging until we're sure they're not suspicious of the horse. Then we shall start again and carry on as we were before. We're just about under the trip-wire now and it would be silly to rush things. We'll rest for a week and then work all-out until we're through.'

'The horse needs re-upholstering,' John said. 'We'll do that during the next week and get our clothing fixed up.'

'What are you wearing?'

'I've got my own brown shoes,' John said, 'and a pair of Australian navy-blue battledress trousers that I swapped for a pair of khaki ones. Jim Strong's lent

97

me his Air Force mackintosh and I've got a beret that I swapped with a Pole in the last camp. All I need really is a jacket of some sort and a civilian shirt and tie.'

'We've managed to get two shirts for you,' Stafford said. 'And I've got a Fleet Air Arm jacket that ought to fit you. Used to belong to my pilot. I'm afraid one sleeve's torn and a bit bloodstained, but if you wash it and take the gold braid off it should pass as a civilian jacket. You can either cover the buttons or replace them.'

'We've got some buttons,' Peter said. 'We've been collecting them for some time.'

'How are you fixed up for clothes?' Stafford turned to Peter.

'Old Tettenborne's got a black B.O.A.C. trench coat – I'm negotiating for that. I shall wear black shoes, and one of the chaps has got a beret made out of a blanket that I can have.'

'What about a suit?'

Peter grinned. 'The Committee have got a phony Marine dress uniform.'

'Yes, I've seen it,' Stafford said. 'It's pretty good.'

'Well, it's hidden somewhere – underground, I think – and they won't let me have it until just before we're ready to go. They say it'll fit me, so I'm trusting to luck and hoping that it will.'

'And what about your papers?'

'They're all in hand. We're going to make for Stettin and try to stow away on a Swedish boat. We shall both travel as French draughtsmen and they're forging our Ausweis and Arbeitskarte now. We shall also have a forged police permission to travel and a letter from our firm in Breslau giving us permission to go. We shall say we're going to the Arado Works at Anklam – just north of Stettin.'

'You know about the Swedish ships being searched, I suppose? They use tear-gas bombs and have specially trained dogs.'

'Yes, we'd heard about that. We thought of taking forged papers and becoming Swedish sailors when we arrive in Stettin – then we could hang around the docks without looking suspicious. We shall each take a dark blue roll-neck sweater so that we can change from foreign workers to Swedish sailors at short notice.'

'Do you know what a Swedish sailor's papers look like?'

'No, we don't, unfortunately, but there's a chap in the camp who was in the Merchant Service and he's going to rough out an English one for us. We shall more or less copy that in Swedish and hope that we shan't need to use it.'

'I still don't like the idea of staying in hotels,' Stafford said.

Peter said nothing but looked obstinate. Stafford recognized this obstinacy – the singleness of purpose that had taken the tunnel this far – and he turned to John.

'I agree with Peter,' John said. 'No one has tried it yet and very few people have got home. Our papers will be good and I think the bolder we are the less suspicious the Germans will be. Besides, it will be October or November before we're out and it's going to be pretty cold sleeping in the open. If we don't get a ship at once – and I don't suppose we will – we'll have to go somewhere at night and I think there's less risk in hotels than in hanging around station waiting-rooms and public lavatories. We've talked the whole thing over and that's what we've decided to do.' He said it with finality.

'Perhaps you're right,' Stafford said. 'I know what it's like to be without a base of some sort. It gets on your nerves, having nowhere to go – no place where you can relax and have a bit of a breather. I've got an address in Stettin. It's a sort of club, but I don't know whether I ought to let you have it.'

'Don't you think we're old enough?' John asked.

'It's not that. I've had the address for some time –

ever since I was out myself, but I never got as far as Stettin – and the place might have been bust wide open by now. They were Polish and they hid Allied prisoners and airmen who were on the loose. But these places are really more of a danger than a help. The Hun might have rumbled it and be using it as a trap.'

'Is it a German club?' Peter asked.

'It's a club for foreign workers. Germans aren't allowed in. But as I say, it might be a trap. I'll give you the address just before you leave the camp. You'll have to commit it to memory. Wouldn't be safe to write it down.'

'We'll remember it,' John said. 'I've never been to a Polish club.'

'What's Rowe doing?' Stafford asked.

'He's going on his own,' Peter said. 'Going to Danzig – travelling as a Swedish commercial traveller.' He smiled now that the need for obstinacy was gone. 'He's practising the role already. He's learning to smoke a pipe so that if he's questioned he can gain time by lighting it.'

'Well, I wish you luck,' Stafford said. 'I think you'll make it. Have a drink on me in Shepherd's, will you?'

'We'll have a drink on you in every pub in town,' Peter promised.

Chapter Eight

Inch By Inch

When they reopened the tunnel at the end of seven days they found that the sand on the roof and walls had dried and considerable falls had occurred. It took them another week to clear the fallen sand and to shore the tunnel in the dangerous places.

It was now early October and the long Silesian summer was ending. All through the summer their working had been controlled by the weather. Once the trap was lifted and the workers were in the tunnel it took them all of fifteen minutes to get back to the shaft, close the trap and get ready to be carried in. They could not afford to be caught out by a shower of rain. If it started to rain the vaulters could not continue without arousing the suspicion of the guards. Nor could they run for the shelter of the canteen leaving the vaulting-horse to stand out in the rain. The obvious thing was to carry the horse in with them, and they could not do this with the trap open and two men in the tunnel. So they studied the weather carefully and if it looked at all like rain they had to vault without digging. Nearly every time they took the horse out it was only after long discussions on the weather. The nearer they got to the wire the more reluctant they were to risk being caught by the rain. They were also determined to be out by the end of October and as the time passed they began to get dogmatic and short-tempered in their discussions.

Philip was more upset than the other two by a sudden change of plan. They would part in the evening having arranged to vault immediately after breakfast the following morning. Philip would arrive in their room, dressed for digging, only to find that owing to a change in the weather they had decided not to dig. Ten minutes afterwards, if the weather showed signs of clearing, they would decide to start work, and all the vaulters would be assembled at a moment's notice.

It was trying for all of them. They were physically tired after three and a half months of digging and now their nerves were becoming frayed by continual anxiety and changes of plan. Peter tried to keep cheerful, but fumed inwardly at the delays caused by the more and more frequent showers of rain.

With the new system of digging the tunnel made slow progress. They had enlarged the end of the tunnel to form a 'bulge' large enough to allow the man working at the face to rest on his elbows and draw his knees up under his chest. Instead of using the usual wooden toboggan for carrying the sand down the tunnel they used a metal basin eighteen inches in diameter and eight inches deep. The basin was just small enough to fit into the tunnel. Two holes had been drilled in opposite sides of the rim of the basin to take the rope which they had plaited from string off the Red Cross parcels.

When the bulge was finished – it took them four days to remove the extra sand – the tunnel was driven on. One man worked in the tunnel extension, dragging the sand backwards into the bulge. Once in the bulge he pulled the basin up the tunnel, past his feet and over his legs on to his stomach, where he filled it with the sand he had brought back. Two pulls on the rope was the signal for the man in the shaft to pull back the basin full of sand. He then tipped the basin over and filled his bags while the worker in the bulge crawled up the tunnel extension for more sand.

At first they merely threaded the rope through the holes in the rim of the basin. But the holes were raggedly punched through with a nail and soon cut the string, leaving the basin stranded – usually halfway up the tunnel. Then there followed a whispered argument as to who was nearer the basin and whose turn it was to crawl up the tunnel and repair the string. Later they made strong wire hooks with which to attach the basin to the rope.

Up to the time of making the bulge they had been troubled by lack of air in the tunnel. Under the new system they found that sufficient air was pushed up the tunnel by the passage of the basin to supply the man in the bulge.

They were now working gradually up towards the surface and it was impossible to remain in the extension for more than a few minutes. If for any reason the basin was not kept moving the shortage of air became dangerous.

After a time they drove the new tunnel so far beyond the bulge that it became impossible to work in the extension and they made a new bulge at the end of the tunnel, filled in the old bulge, lengthened the rope and carried on as before. They made three such bulges before the tunnel was complete.

Try as they might they could not persuade Philip to enter the tunnel in the nude. He insisted on wearing a shirt, shorts and tennis shoes; and for this reason they did all they could to arrange that he remained in the shaft.

It was a feat of some endurance to drag the thirty-odd full basins of sand from the face to the shaft. In addition to this the bags had to be filled and lifted one by one and stacked inside the vaulting-horse. So Peter and John pleaded fatigue and persuaded Philip to allow one of them to work at the face whenever it was his turn to dig.

When they had been digging for some months John became convinced that the tunnel was veering to the left. Peter, who was in charge of the construction, was convinced that the tunnel was straight. They had taken their direction by a home-made compass. After considerable argument they decided to put it to the test.

Peter crawled to the end of the tunnel with the rope of the basin tied to his ankle. He took with him a thin metal poker about four feet long. John sat in the shaft holding the other end of the rope while Nigel sat on the horse apparently resting after an energetic bout of vaulting.

Philip stood gazing out through the wire, hands in pockets, in the hopeless, forlorn and typically Kriegie attitude. Prisoners strolled slowly round the wire. The guards brooded in their boxes. The whole camp wore its usual afternoon air of lassitude.

Peter, lying full length at the end of the tunnel, scooped a deep pit in the floor in front of his face. He placed the end of the poker in the pit and forced it slowly upwards through the roof of the tunnel, using a corkscrew motion to avoid bringing down the roof. It was hard work. Steady trickles of sand fell from the ceiling, covering his head and shoulders. Inch by inch he forced the poker upwards until the end was flush with the ceiling of the tunnel. He scraped the sand away from around the poker and pushed it up still higher. By the sudden lack of resistance he knew that it was through and protruding above the surface of the ground. He gave two tugs on the rope to tell John that he was through. John knocked on the inside of the horse and Nigel, hearing this, sent a messenger across to Philip.

Philip, without appearing to do so, frantically scanned the ground in front of him for the end of the poker. He could not see it.

Peter became impatient and began to move the poker slowly up and down. Then Philip saw it. He scratched his head. Nigel kicked the side of the horse. John pulled the rope and Peter pulled down the poker.

The end of the tunnel was under the wire, but fifteen feet to the left of where Peter had expected it to be.

The following morning Peter, John and Philip walked together round the wire completing their plans for the break.

'We shall have to "mole" the last ten feet,' Peter said. 'We're under the wire now and we've twelve days to go to the end of the month. If we're lucky we shall do another six feet by then. That puts us about three feet outside the wire. There's a shallow ditch about twelve feet beyond the wire and if we can manage to strike that it will give us some cover for the break.'

'It's still in the light of the arc lamps,' John objected.

'The light from the lamps extends for about thirty feet outside the wire and we can't possibly push the tunnel on as far as that. Besides, the only railway timetable Stafford's got expires at the end of the month and we *must* time the break so that we just have time to leap down to the station and catch a train. If we get out and then have to hang about waiting for a train we stand a good chance of getting picked up right away.'

'I agree with Pete,' Philip said. 'We'll just have to organize a diversion in the huts nearest the wire at the time that we mean to break.'

'That won't be too easy,' John said. 'Who's going to estimate how long it's going to take us to mole ten feet?'

'We'll have to over-estimate it,' Peter said. 'Then add half as much time again, and if we reach the ditch before the time we've said – we'll just have to lie doggo until we hear the diversion start.' He turned to Philip. 'Will you organize the diversion?'

'O.K. I'll get that laid on. What about the outside sentries?'

'They don't come on until an hour after dusk. John and I have been sitting up all night watching them. There are two on the side where we are. They each patrol half the wire, meet in the middle, turn back to back and walk to the end. If it's raining they stand under a tree. They walk pretty slowly and when the diversion starts they and the goons in the boxes will be looking inwards towards the noise. We should get past them all right.' He spoke confidently, but thought of tommy-gun bullets and the sharp cry in the night when Alan had been shot on the wire. 'We shall have to wear dark clothes,' he said.

'I'd thought of that,' Philip said. 'We've just had some

long woollen combinations sent in by the Red Cross. If we dye them black with tea-leaves or coffee we could put them on over our clothes. It will keep us clean while we're down there and be good camouflage when we get out.'

'John and I thought of going down naked,' Peter said.

'*I'm* not going to get caught and dragged off to the cooler without a stitch of clothing. It's all right for you nudists. Besides, my skin's not like yours – it's too white and would show up too much. There's another thing too – I want to go right along that hole tomorrow and have a look at the end. I don't trust you two. I want to make certain it's big enough to take me and all my kit.'

'What's all this talk of "all my kit"?' John asked.

'Well, I'm going as a commercial traveller, aren't I? I shall need a bag of samples and I've got a black Homburg hat I bribed off one of the goons. That will have to go in a box to save it from getting crushed. Then I'm wearing an R.A.F. greatcoat . . .'

'He'd better go down tomorrow and see how big the hole is,' John said.

'Right,' Peter said, 'but look here, Phil, none of your little games. No widening it while you're down there and saying it fell in. It's quite big enough as it is.'

'Let's get this thing straight,' Philip said. 'You can't go down there naked – you'll have to wear shoes at least in case you have to run. And I wouldn't fancy running through those woods with dogs after me without any clothes on.'

'We must remember to get some pepper for the dogs,' Peter said.

'Yes, but what about the kit?'

'I like the idea of the combinations,' John said. 'We could wear socks over our shoes and black hoods over our heads.'

106

'We shan't be able to wear all our clothes,' Peter said. 'The hole's not big enough.'

'We'll wear our shirts and trousers then,' Philip said, 'and pack the rest of our kit in kitbags dyed black. We can drag them down the tunnel tied to our ankles.'

'We haven't solved the most important problem yet,' Peter said.

'What's that?'

'How to get four people out in the horse.'

'Four people?' Philip sounded excited. 'I thought only we three were going!'

'Yes, but somebody's got to close the trap down after us.'

'Do you mean to say that you haven't arranged all that?' Philip was even more excited.

'As a matter of fact I never thought we'd get as far as we have.' Peter winked at John. 'When we decided to ask you to come in we never considered how we were going to get out once the tunnel was finished. We could have got three into the horse at a pinch, but I'm darned if I can see how we could get four.'

'We'll have to draw lots,' John said.

Philip nearly choked. 'D'you mean to say that you've got as far as this and never considered how we were to get out?'

'Did *you* consider it?' Peter asked.

'I thought you'd got it all fixed.'

'We'll have to put the kit down the day before,' John said.

'We can't do that,' Peter said. 'If we put three kitbags in the tunnel we shan't be able to get down ourselves.'

'Then we'll have to make a chamber near the end of the tunnel large enough to take them.'

'That's a week's work in itself,' Peter said. 'I can't see us finishing up much outside the wire. We've got to get past the path where the outside sentries walk and we've

107

got to do it before the end of the month. Our timetable expires at the end of the month and after that goodness knows how the trains will run.'

'Pray God it doesn't rain much during the next few days,' Philip said.

'We'll just have to vault in the rain, that's all. The goons think we're mad already. We'll just have to risk it and hope they don't get suspicious.'

'What train do you and John want to catch?'

'There's a fast train to Frankfurt at six-thirty p.m. German time,' Peter said. 'It's dark by five-thirty and the outside guards usually come on soon after that. If we break at six o'clock it will be dark enough and we stand a chance of getting out before the guards arrive. We don't want to go too early because if they find the hole and get to the station before the train goes we'll get picked up.'

'That train will do me too,' Philip said.

'You're definitely not coming with us then?' Peter asked. It's just as well, he thought. We'd only row if we all went together. Old Phil's much better on his own. He'll make his plans and he'll stick to them, which is something we'd never do. Ours is the better way though. Keep it fluid. You need less luck our way. And we can do it . . .

'I'll go on my own,' Philip said. 'I'll make for Danzig and try to get a boat there.'

'We shall get off at Frankfurt,' John said. 'Take the fast train as far as Frankfurt, spend the night there, and see how things go. We shall most likely make Stettin in two or three short hops. Most likely we shall get off before we get to Stettin station and walk into the town.'

'I shall go straight on up to Danzig,' Philip said. 'I hope to be in Sweden three days after leaving the camp.'

'I think you're doing the right thing,' Peter said. 'The

right thing for you. Speaking German and travelling as a neutral, a long-distance fast train is the obvious thing. You should get away with it. Once we get to Frankfurt we shall go by slow local trains.'

'I think I've got it!' John said.

'Got what?' Peter asked.

'If I go down in the afternoon before roll-call – say about two o'clock in the afternoon – and take the baggage with me, you can seal me down and I'll dig the whole of the afternoon. You can cook my absence at roll-call and then you two come down as soon as you can. Roll-call's at three forty-five, so you'll be down about four o'clock, or soon after. You can take someone out with you – the smallest man we can find – to seal the trap down after you, and then we'll have two hours in which to get ready to break.'

'It'll be pretty grim,' Peter said, 'stuck down there alone for a couple of hours.'

'Oh, I shall be all right. I'll put an air-hole up inside the wire where it won't be seen, and mole on quite happily. I should do five or six feet before you come down.'

'Don't go and overdo it.' Peter knew John's unsparing energy once he'd set his heart to a thing. He was all energy once he started. Nervous energy and guts. He took more out of himself than he knew. 'Remember we may have to run for it,' he said. 'Don't fag yourself out digging – leave most of it for when we get down there.'

'Oh, I'll take it easy,' John lied. Peter knew he lied and could do nothing about it.

'That's everything then, is it?' Philip asked. 'I'll go along and see the Committee and fix up the diversion for six o'clock. I want to see about my samples too.'

'What are they?' Peter asked.

'Samples of margarine packed in wooden boxes,' Philip replied. 'I'll eat them if I get hungry.'

Chapter Nine

The Break-Out

For the next twelve days they vaulted every day and removed as much sand as they could. They increased the number of bags to fourteen and finally fifteen, although the bearers staggered as they carried the horse into the canteen.

On October the twenty-eighth they made the final bulge at the end of the tunnel. This was as far as they could go. They reckoned that between them they could dig a further ten feet after they had been sealed down. The bulge they made to hold their kitbags while they were digging the last ten feet and finally breaking through to the surface.

They spent the next morning bringing in the last twelve bags and recovering their civilian clothing from their various scattered hiding places round the camp. At twelve-thirty John had his last meal, a substantial meal of bully beef, potatoes and Canadian biscuits and cheese. At one o'clock he went over to the canteen with the camp glee-singing club. He wore his civilian clothes under a long khaki Polish greatcoat. Earlier in the day their baggage had been taken to the canteen, hidden in bundles of dirty laundry.

While John was eating the last of his lunch Peter went along to see the duty pilot. There were two ferrets in the compound. Bother, he thought, they would have to be here now. 'Where are they?' he asked.

'One's in the kitchen, the other's hanging around outside the canteen.'

Peter thought for a moment. 'O.K.,' he said. 'If any more come into the compound send a stooge off to Philip. He'll be in the canteen.'

He ran across to the S.B.O.; knocked on the door. 'Come in.'

He stood in the doorway, panting slightly. 'Sir – we're just putting Clinton down and there's a goon hanging round the canteen. I wonder if you could get him out of the way for a few minutes?'

The S.B.O. smiled and put down his book. 'Let me see,' he said, 'the cooking stove in Hut 64 isn't drawing very well. I'll just stroll over and ask him to have a look at it. He might like to smoke an English cigarette in my room.'

'Thank you, sir.'

Back at the canteen he found the glee-club singing an old English folk song. John, Philip, Nigel and the vaulters were standing near the door.

'We can't get started,' John said. 'There's a ferret outside and he keeps walking past and looking in at the window. I don't think he likes the singing.'

'It'd be worse without it,' Peter said. 'There's another next door in the kitchen. The S.B.O. is going to take the one outside away and then we'll get cracking.' He looked out of the window. The S.B.O. was walking across the Sportsplatz, a golf club in his hand. Suddenly he appeared to see the ferret and altered course. 'Here comes "Groupy,"' Peter said. 'Good man!'

The group captain exchanged a few words with the ferret and they both walked away across the Sportsplatz.

'O.K.,' said Peter. 'Let's go!'

John hurriedly doffed his coat and pulled the long black combinations on over his clothes. He pulled black socks over his shoes and adjusted the hood which was made from an old under-vest dyed black. 'It's pretty hot in here,' he said.

111

'You look like the Ku Klux Klan in reverse,' Peter told him. 'O.K.?'

They both crawled under the vaulting-horse, Peter holding a blanket, a cardboard box and twelve empty bags; John sinister in his black clothes. The three kitbags hung between them suspended from the top of the horse. They both crouched with their backs to the ends of the horse, their feet one each side on the bottom framework. Then the bearing poles were inserted and the horse was raised. Tightly holding the kitbags to prevent them from swaying, they lurched down the steps and went creaking across the compound towards the vaulting-pits.

With a sigh of relief the bearers placed the horse in position and withdrew the poles ready for vaulting.

John crouched in one end of the horse while Peter piled the kitbags on top of him. Peter then spread the blanket on the ground at the other end of the horse and began to uncover the trap. He first collected the grey top layer in the cardboard box and threw the damp subsoil on to the blanket. Feeling round with his fingers he uncovered the bags of sand on top of the trap. He scraped the sand away from the damp wood. As he removed the trap he smelled the familiar damp musty smell of the tunnel. He lifted the kitbags off John's crouching figure and balanced them on top of the trap on the pile of sand. 'Down you go,' he said, and crouched astride the hole while John dropped feet first into the shaft. 'Whew, those clothes stink!'

'It'll be worse by the time you come down,' John said. 'It's the dye. Must have gone bad or something.'

While John crawled up the tunnel Peter detached the metal basin from the end of the rope and tied one of the kitbags in its place. One by one John pulled the kitbags up the tunnel and put them in the bulge at the end. Peter then replaced the basin and between them they filled the twelve empty bags they had taken out with them.

While Peter was stacking the bags in the body of the

horse, John crawled back for his last breath of fresh air. It was the first time he had been in the tunnel wearing clothes and Peter could hear him cursing softly as he struggled to get back. Finally his feet came into view and then his body, clothed and clumsy under the black combinations. Peter crouched inside the horse looking down on him as he emerged. Outside he could hear the shouting of the vaulters and the reverberating concussion as they landed on top of the horse. John straightened up, head and shoulders out of the trap. He had left the hood at the end of the tunnel and his face was red.

'It's pretty hot down there with clothes on.'

'Take it easy,' Peter said. 'For goodness' sake don't overdo it. I don't want to have to carry you once we get outside.'

'I'll be all right. You seal me down now and I'll see you later.'

'O.K., but for goodness' sake don't make the air-hole bigger than you have to.' Peter said.

He watched John's legs disappear down the narrow tunnel and then he replaced the trap. He replaced the heavy bags of sand and stamped the loose sand firmly on top of them. It's burying a man alive, he thought. Then he heard an anxious voice from outside.

'How's it going, Pete?'

'Five minutes, Phil,' he said, and started to hang the twelve bags of sand from the top of the horse. He gathered the blanket in his arms and spread the rest of the sand evenly over the ground under the horse. He sprinkled the dry grey sand from the cardboard box over this and gave Philip a low hail that he was ready. The bearing poles were inserted and he was carried back into the canteen.

As they neared the canteen he could hear the voices of the male voice choir. 'He shall set His angels guard over thee . . . Lest thou catch thy foot against a stone . . .' He grinned widely in the dark belly of the horse.

With a final creaking lurch they were up the steps and inside the canteen. The old horse is falling to pieces, Peter thought. Hope it lasts out this evening.

One end of the horse was lifted and he passed the bags of sand out to Philip. Between them they carried the bags into the band practice room where the choir was going at full blast. 'He shall set His angels, there's a ferret outside the window,' sang David.

'O.K.,' said Peter. 'Keep an eye on him. Is Nig in the roof?'

David nodded his head and continued singing.

'Right. We'll just get these bags to safety in the roof and then we're O.K.'

Nigel's anxious face was peering down from the trap door in the ceiling. Peter held out his fist, thumb extended upwards, and grinned. Nigel grinned too, and lowered his arm for the first of the bags.

Roll-call was at three forty-five and Peter and Philip spent the time until then lying on their bunks. For Peter this was the worst moment of all. This waiting after the work had been done. This lying on his bunk while John was down below digging, and at any moment the scheme might blow and their four and a half months' effort be wasted. Once they were outside he felt it wouldn't matter so much. He hardly expected to get back to England. That was looking too far ahead. That was too much in the lap of the gods. Anything might happen once they were outside. Outside the wire they would rely almost entirely on their luck. It was no use making detailed plans of what they would do when they were outside. They could make a rough outline plan of what they wanted to do, but that was all. From the moment they left the end of the tunnel they would have to adapt their policy to the conditions they met. He could not plan ahead a single day.

And so he lay on his back on the bunk and let his

mind run over the list of things he was taking with him.

There was the 'dog food,' a hard cake made from dried milk, sugar, Bemax and cocoa. It had been packed in small square tins from the Red Cross parcels and he intended to wear a girdle of them between two shirts.

Next there were several linen bags containing a dry mixture of oatmeal, raisins, sugar and milk powder. When they ate this it would swell in the stomach and prevent that hollow aching sickness that comes from eating ill-balanced concentrated food. He had sewn one of these bags into each armpit of his jacket as an emergency ration if he became separated from the attaché case which held the bulk of their food.

The attaché case was already down in the tunnel, at the bottom of the kitbag. He mentally checked its contents: the food, clean socks, shaving gear, a roll-neck sweater, soap, a small packet of paper and pen and ink for minor alterations to their papers, and spare cigarettes and matches.

He got to his feet and checked over his jacket pockets. The wallet which held his papers and German money, a small pocket compass, a penknife, handkerchiefs, his pipe (a German one bought in the town by one of the guards), a length of string, a pencil, a German tobacco pouch, his beret and a comb.

He went out on the circuit. It was no use, he couldn't be still. He walked round, over the tunnel, and thought of John moling away down there, sweating away, not knowing the time, not knowing whether the tunnel had been discovered, out of touch with everyone. John digging away, trying to get as much done as he could before the others joined him.

He checked with Philip on the timing of the diversion for their break, and then walked with Nigel several times round the circuit while they waited for the appel.

'I shall miss you after you've gone,' Nigel said. 'It's been quite good fun, this vaulting.'

'I expect they'll take the horse away when they discover the tunnel,' Peter said. He wanted to thank Nigel for all the help he had given, but he knew that he could not do it. To thank him would put the thing on a formal basis and it was beyond that. So they walked, trying to talk naturally, and waited for the roll-call.

At roll-call the Senior British Officer, suitably disguised, took John's place in the ranks and his absence was not noticed.

As soon as roll-call was finished the vaulters assembled at the canteen. Peter's knees felt loose and he did not want to go in the horse. They had taken it out twice already that day and he felt that the third time would be unlucky. It was the first time they had vaulted after evening roll-call and he was certain that the guards would be suspicious. As he pulled on the evil-smelling black combinations he could hear Nigel instructing the four men who were to carry the horse. He looked at Philip, unrecognizable in his black hood; and then at the third man, a New Zealander called McKay, whom they had chosen as the lightest man in the camp. He was stripped for lightness and holding the cardboard box for the dry sand to be sprinkled over the trap after he had sealed them down.

Nigel came in and handed him a bottle of cold tea for John. 'Give him my love,' he said, 'and tell him to write.'

Peter and Philip crawled under the horse, stood one at each end and held McKay suspended between them. The poles were placed in position and the horse protestingly started on its last journey. One of the bearers slipped as they came down the steps and Peter thought he would drop them. The man recovered his balance and they went swaying and jerking across the football pitch.

Once the horse was in position Philip sat on McKay's

116

back at one end while Peter again removed the trap. As he took out the wooden boards he listened for sounds of movement in the tunnel. It was silent. He looked at Philip.

'I'll go up the tunnel and see how John is,' he said. 'You fill twelve bags from the bottom of the shaft for Mac to take back, and then stay down this end. I'll send the sand back to you in the basin and you spread it along the floor of the tunnel as you come up.'

'Right.'

'You'll never get down there!' McKay looked with wonder at the narrowness of the shaft.

Peter dropped feet first into the vertical shaft. He slid to his knees, edging his legs backwards into the back burrow. Stooping awkwardly in his tight clothing, he managed to get his head under the lintel of the opening and slipped head first into the tunnel. He waved his legs in farewell, and squirmed inch by inch along the hundred feet that had taken them so long to build. Now that it was finished he was almost sorry. The tunnel had been first in his thoughts for months, cherished, nursed; and now it was finished and he was crawling down it for the last time.

He had brought the torch with him and as he inched along he could see heaps of loose sand dislodged by John's clothing. He noticed all the patches of shoring, strangely unfamiliar in the light but which had been built with difficulty in darkness.

As he neared the end of the tunnel he flashed the torch ahead and called softly to John. He was afraid to call loudly for he was now under the wire and close to the sentry's beat. He passed the bend where they had altered course, and came to the end of the tunnel.

Where he had expected to find John there was nothing but a solid wall of sand.

John must have been digging steadily on and in banking up the sand behind him had completely blocked the tunnel.

117

Peter bored a small hole through the wall of sand which was about three feet thick. As he broke through a gust of hot fetid air gushed out and there was John, wringing wet with perspiration and black from head to foot with the dye that had run out of his combinations. Sand clung to his face where he had sweated and his hair, caked with sand, fell forward over his eyes. He looked pale and tired under the yellow light of Peter's torch.

'Where on earth have you been?' he asked.

'It's only just about four-thirty,' Peter said.

'I thought it must have gone six. I seem to have been down here for hours. I thought the roll-call had gone wrong and I'd have to go out alone.'

'It's all O.K.,' Peter said. 'I've got a bottle of tea here.' He pushed it through the hole to John. 'I'll just send this sand back to Phil and then I'll join you.' He pulled the empty basin up the tunnel and sent the first load back to Philip, who filled the empty bags he had brought down and stacked them in the shaft.

As they worked on they found that now the end of the tunnel where Peter and John were working had a certain amount of fresh air from the air-hole under the wire. Philip, with the trap sealed down, had none.

They worked feverishly trying to get as much as possible done before the breaking time. John, in front, stabbing at the face with the trowel and pushing the damp sand under his belly back towards Peter, who lay with his head on John's heels collecting the sand and squirming backwards with it to Philip, who banked it up as a solid wall behind him.

They were now in a narrow portion of the tunnel about twenty-five feet long and two feet square, ventilated by one small hole three inches in diameter.

They were working for the first time in clothes and for the first time without the fresh air pushed up the tunnel by the basin. They were working three in the tunnel and they were anxious about the air. They were working for the first time by the light of a torch, and in this light the tunnel seemed smaller and the earth above more solid. The prisoners had been locked in for the night and if the tunnel collapsed now they were helpless.

They all worked fast and steadily. None of them wanted to be the one to break the rhythm of the work.

At five-thirty Peter, who had a watch, called a halt. 'We'd better push up to the top now,' he whispered. 'We've got to be out in half an hour.'

John nodded his agreement and began to push the tunnel up towards the surface. It was farther than they had expected and they thought they would never get to the top. Finally, John broke through – a hole as large as his fist – and through it he caught his first glimpse of the stars. The stars in the free heavens beyond the wire.

'I'll break out the whole width of the tunnel,' John whispered, 'just leaving the thin crust over the top. Then we can break that quickly and there'll be less chance of being seen.'

Peter squeezed his arm in reply and squirmed back to Philip to warn him to get ready. On his way back he brought John's kitbag which Philip had tied to his ankle. He then went back for his own. Philip pushed his along the tunnel in front of his nose.

At exactly six o'clock they broke through to the open air, pulling the dry sandy surface down on top of them, choking and blinding them and making them want to cough. As they broke through they heard the sound of the diversion coming from the huts nearest the wire. There were men blowing trumpets, men singing, men banging the sides of the hut and yelling at the top of their voices.

'The silly asses will get a bullet in there if they're not careful,' John whispered.

'Go on! Go now!' Peter said. He was scared. It was too light.

Quickly John hoisted his kitbag out of the tunnel and rolled it towards the ditch. He squeezed himself out of the hole and Peter saw his legs disappear from view.

Peter stuck his head out of the tunnel and looked towards the camp. It was brilliantly floodlit. He had not realized how brilliantly it was lit. But the raised sentry boxes were in darkness and he could not see whether the guards were looking in his direction or not. He could not see the guards outside the wire. He lifted out his kitbag and pushed it towards the ditch, wriggling himself out of the hole and rolling full length on the ground towards the ditch. He expected every minute to hear the crack of a rifle and feel the tearing impact of its bullet in his flesh. He gained the ditch and lay listening. The diversion in the huts had reached a new crescendo of noise.

He picked up his kitbag and ran blindly towards the pine forest on the other side of the road where John was waiting for him.

Phase Two

Chapter One

A Night In The Open

Once they reached the edge of the wood they did not wait for Philip but walked slowly away from the wire, towards the centre of the forest. Peter could feel his heart thumping high up inside his chest, choking him. He wanted to run but forced himself to walk slowly, feeling with his feet for the dry branches that lay among the pine needles on the forest floor. His tunnelling clothes were wet with perspiration and the keen wind cut through them. He was cold now and anxious to get into the shelter of the forest where they could dress. Looking backwards over his shoulder he saw the compound through the trees, floodlit like some giant circus. There had been no shots and he knew that Philip was safely away behind them somewhere in the forest.

He stopped and stood looking backwards at the bright lights among the trees.

'It's a piece of cake,' John whispered. 'Come on, Pete. We'll have to move if we're going to catch that train.'

But Peter stood for a moment gazing back at the camp that he hoped never to see again; the camp that he hated but which held so many of his friends.

John caught him by the arm and they walked on into the forest, moving carefully on the loose and noisy ground.

John started laughing under his breath. First giggles and then long gusts of low, shaking, uncontrollable mirth.

'What's the matter?' Pete whispered. 'What the devil's the matter? What the devil are you laughing at?'

'It's you . . .' John said, 'you look like some great bear mincing along like that . . .'

Peter was carrying the kitbag baby-like in his arms.

'Let's get out of these combinations,' John said. 'Let's get cleaned up and look like human beings.'

'Not yet. Lay the trail away from the railway station. We'll hide them on the side of the road to Breslau.' Peter, too, was laughing, laughing with the release of strained nerves and with the triumph of escape. But he was not yet relaxed. His laughter was brittle, nervous.

They picked their way carefully through the forest until they were out of earshot of the camp. They were trembling now, cold in their thin woollen combinations, cold and tired by the digging; but not feeling tired. Not feeling tired because they were free, outside the wire that had held them for so long.

Ahead of them the pine forest stretched silent and unbroken for miles. It stretched almost unbroken into Jugoslavia. But it was a winter forest. A forest of bare branches and tall silent trees, unfriendly and inhospitable. They had been in the forest before and knew its inhospitality. A short mile away was the railway station, crowded and risky, but holding the promise of a rapid journey to the coast.

They stripped off the black combination suits and the socks from over their shoes. They washed one another's faces with their handkerchiefs and took their civilian jackets, hats and mackintoshes from the kitbags.

At the bottom of the kitbags they each had a small travelling bag. Peter opened his and took out a tin of pepper. He put the clothing together in a heap and sprinkled it liberally with the pepper, holding his nose as he did it.

They put on their mackintoshes and berets and doubled

back towards the railway, making straight for the bridge that led to the station. It was a high metal footbridge over the railway line. They crossed it and gained the road on the other side.

'Walk on the right-hand side,' Peter said. 'Then we shan't be facing the oncoming traffic.'

There were several people on the road. A local train had evidently just pulled in. Hope they're not waiting at the station, Peter thought. Hope the alarm hasn't gone and we don't find a crowd of guards waiting at the station.

'If we're recognized we'll cut and run,' he said. 'They won't shoot with all these people about. We'll separate. I'll meet you by the water tower in the forest, and we'll walk, or jump goods trains. If they know we're out all the stations for miles around will be watched.'

'It's O.K.,' John said. 'We shan't get caught. If the alarm had gone we'd have heard it. Just look slap-happy. We'll be O.K.'

Outside the station it was dark, but inside the booking hall the lights were bright. Peter walked to the timetable on the wall while John joined the queue at the booking office. He had Peter's identity card and police permission to travel.

Peter turned to watch him as he stood in the queue. To him the Air Force trench coat was glaringly obvious. But the beret and John's lean dark face looked French enough. A young slim figure in a beret and grey-blue trench coat carrying the travelling-bag he had made himself out of a canvas valise. He looked unconcerned as he stood in the queue waiting his turn at the booking-office window; but Peter saw him draw in his underlip and guessed at his feelings as he stood there waiting.

He was at the window now, talking to the girl behind the grille. Peter looked towards the door. It was crowded with people. I'll wait until he gets within about three feet of me and then we'll both charge together, he thought. We'll get through that lot all right. He turned again towards John. He was coming over to him with the tickets in his hand. Peter joined him and they stood together at the barrier waiting for the passengers to leave the platform before they went through.

Peter stood watching the passengers as they came out through the barrier. His heart pounded. He wanted to run. Coming through the barrier was the doctor who had been treating him in hospital. They had talked every day for a week and he was bound to be recognized. Then he remembered that he had removed his beard the night before. As the Hauptmann came by, within a foot of him, Peter stopped and fumbled with the fastener of his attaché case. When he looked up the Hauptmann had passed and John was pushing him towards the barrier on to the platform.

They walked up and down the platform waiting for the train. They had ten minutes to wait. They walked to the end of the platform and studied the lie of the land.

'If the alarm goes before the train gets in, we'll jump on to the line and down that embankment,' Peter said. 'We'll circle round the town and if we get separated we'll meet at the water tower.'

'We'll hear the camp sirens all right from here,' John said. 'Wait until the last minute in case the train gets in before they get here.' He sounded confident.

'No,' said Peter, not liking this confidence, not wanting it to be too easy. 'No – we'll go as soon as we hear the sirens. If they find out we've gone it'll be no use catching the train. They'll telephone Frankfurt and catch us there. It'll be better to get right away from the railway and get into the country.'

'We could catch the train and jump it before we got to Frankfurt.'

'It wouldn't be worth it. The train might be late and

126

then we'd be caught on the platform. If we hear the sirens we'll get off right away and take to the woods.'

'O.K.,' John said. 'We'll be O.K.'

The train was crowded and in darkness. They stood in the corridor. Peter stood near the door looking out of the window and listening to the rat-a-tat-tat of the wheels. Every minute is taking us farther away, he thought. We're going to make it. He looked round him for John. They had become separated and John was squeezed in between a burly German soldier and an old woman. He was leaning back against the side of the carriage with his eyes closed.

They stood like this all the way to Frankfurt. It was ten-thirty when they arrived and they hurried towards the barrier to see what check there was before the crowd dispersed. The passengers were not being asked to show their papers – they were merely handing in their tickets. Peter walked towards the barrier, but John pulled him back and steered him towards another exit farther away. Peter said nothing but followed him. They passed the barrier and stood safely outside in the spacious booking hall.

'Why did you pull me back?' Peter whispered.

'That one was for soldiers only, you ass. Come on, let's get out of the station and on to the street.' He wanted to get away; to get Peter away from the bright lights of the station. Away from the danger of the bright lights and the people.

They left the booking hall and walked out into the darkness of the cobbled streets – the strange foreign streets of which they had no experience. In which nothing was familiar, with signposts and shop signs in a foreign tongue. Nowhere to sleep. Strange after the close confinement of the prison camp and exciting to be walking along the streets of a town, fugitives surrounded by enemies and unable to speak more than a few words of the language.

127

Peter stuck close to John and together they made for the centre of the town.

They stopped outside a large hotel. 'Let's go in and ask for a room,' John said.

Peter hesitated.

'We've got to do it sooner or later,' John urged. 'It's nearly eleven o'clock and I don't suppose they'll have one. Better do it now, late at night when the porter's tired. We'll see how he reacts.'

'It's not worth it,' Peter said. 'Let's sleep in the country.'

'Snap out of it,' John said. 'We decided against the country months ago. The railway was O.K. and the hotels are going to be O.K. too.'

It was a large hotel which would, in England, have been of the Victorian period, but it had been modernized. The walls of the entrance hall were covered in green plastic paint and there was a carpet of modern design on the floor. Several people were sitting in a lounge on the left of the entrance hall.

John went straight up to the hall porter's desk at the far end of the room. He spoke respectfully but with confidence, adopting the role of a member of a defeated nation, but a free worker and not an ex-prisoner of war.

'*Haben Sie, bitte, ein Doppel-Zimmer frei?*'

The porter said something Peter did not understand. John thanked the man and moved towards the door. Peter followed him out on to the street.

'What did he say?' he asked.

'He said all the rooms were taken.'

'I don't like it,' Peter said. 'We don't even know if foreign workers are allowed to stay in hotels. Did he seem surprised when you asked?'

'I don't think so. I don't see why foreign workers shouldn't stay in hotels.'

'They do some funny things in Germany. They have

128

separate clubs for the foreign workers. I don't see why they shouldn't have separate hotels too.'

'We'll try a smaller hotel next time,' John said. 'Let's go back to the station. The cheaper hotels are usually near the station.'

They tried four more hotels and finally found themselves back outside the railway station.

'This is worse than London,' John said. 'What do we do now?'

'Let's get out into the country,' Peter suggested. 'Let's walk out of the town and sleep under a hedge.'

They walked for two hours, passing from the industrial city through an area of fine, large houses into the suburbs. They passed through the suburbs and finally came out on to a country lane running between flat fields.

'This is as far as I go,' John said.

'We can't sleep here,' Peter said. 'We must find some sort of cover.'

'I'm tired. I must sleep.'

'Let's walk a bit more. We're bound to find a barn or something soon.'

'I don't care what it is as long as I sleep.'

John was finished now. Finished with the digging, the bad air and the strain. They walked on, John stumbling and muttering to himself about sleep. Sleep on a hard bench or even on the gravel by the side of the road. His eyes were pricking as though there was sand under the lids, and his mouth was dry.

They came to a large house standing back from the road, a fine brick house with a high-pitched roof. A typical, angular German farm. There was a notice fixed to one of the brick gate pillars. John stood close to the gate trying to read the notice which was surmounted by a cross.

'It's a Kloster,' he said. 'A convent. I wonder if they'd give us sanctuary.'

129

'Not in Germany. In France or Holland perhaps, but not in Germany. Imagine an escaping German prisoner going to an English convent and asking for sanctuary. No, it's no use asking for help in Germany. Let's walk on.'

They walked on down the road looking for a suitable place to hide up for the night. Finally Peter pointed out a concrete drain running through a deep ditch and passing as a tunnel under the road.

'Let's go down there,' he said.

They climbed down the weed- and scrub-covered slope and found a secluded spot hidden from the road above. They opened their bags and ate the sandwiches they had brought with them from the camp.

'Tomorrow we start on the dog food,' Peter said.

When they had eaten they settled down to sleep. They slept just as they were, in their mackintoshes and their shoes, their heads on their bags, side by side on the rough damp ground.

An hour later Peter woke shivering. He was wearing thick woollen underclothes, two shirts, a sweater, a naval uniform and mackintosh; and he woke shivering. He rose quietly to his feet, afraid of waking John, but John was already awake.

'Let's put my mackintosh on the ground to lie on and put yours over us,' John said.

They swung their arms to restore the circulation and did as he suggested. They fell asleep again huddled together for warmth, but they woke later because their backs were cold. So they lay back to back and slept fitfully until just before dawn.

Chapter Two

The Train Check

They left their hiding place before it was light and after cleaning one another down they walked back the way they had come, into the town. It was still dark in the streets, but everywhere the German people were hurrying to their work.

As they came into the town they met the early morning trams and by the time they reached the railway station it was almost light. The booking hall was crowded and Peter followed John as he threaded his way towards the notice board. He felt safer as part of this early morning crowd, less vulnerable than when they were walking in the open street.

John stood looking at the board for some minutes, then turned and made towards a less crowded part of the hall.

'There's a train for Küstrin in an hour's time,' he said. 'It's a local stopping train.'

'We'll take that,' Peter said. 'Let's go and try to get a cup of coffee to warm us up a bit.'

'We don't know if it's rationed – but after all we're supposed to be foreigners. Can't be expected to know everything.'

'We mustn't go to the Red Cross stalls on the platform,' Peter told him. 'They're for troops only.'

'How do you know that?'

'Got it off one of the guards in the hospital. Started boasting about our Red Cross and he unbuttoned and told me all about theirs.'

The waiting-room was warm and crowded and smelled strongly of German cigarettes. They found a place at one of the tables and sat there awkwardly, not talking. It was difficult to sit there not talking and yet look natural.

Peter looked round him at the people sitting at the tables. They were mostly in uniform and seemed uninterested in the two young Frenchmen sitting silently in the middle of the room. He took out a blue paper packet of cigarettes and offered them to John. John took one and thanked him in fluent French. Peter grinned in outward comprehension, shrugging his shoulders in what he hoped was the French manner.

They had been sitting there for some time before Peter realized that there were no waiters. It was a 'help-yourself' counter. John's back was to the counter and he had not seen it. Peter could not speak so he kicked John's foot, but John only smiled reassuringly. Peter picked up a newspaper from the chair next to him and appeared to study it. He took the pencil from his pocket and wrote in the margin NO WAITERS - HELP YOURSELF, and passed the paper to John who tore the margin from the paper, folded it and put it in his pocket. He yawned elaborately and looked at his watch. Then he said something in French and walked over to the counter.

The coffee was ersatz and not very hot. It was made from acorns – the same brand that had been issued in Dulag-Luft. The rations weren't so bad, I suppose, Peter thought. Coming straight from an English standard they seemed foul enough – but by their own standard I suppose they weren't so bad. He looked round him at the workmen and soldiers sitting at the tables. None of them was eating. None of them looked very fit. He looked at John. We look too fit, he thought, although if we were looking for an escaped prisoner in England I shouldn't go for a very fit-looking man. Have to shave soon. He ran his hand under his chin. It'll do. It'll do today anyway. Like to clean my teeth too. Daren't go to a wash-and-brush-up place – too intimate. Have to stick it, I suppose. Wonder what John's thinking about? Looks a bit strained. Wish I could do more to help. Pretty useless not knowing the lingo. Must be a devil of a strain doing all the talking. I'll try to do all the worrying about policy and let him do the talking. He's good though – looks more French than the French. Wonder if I look French? More like an Italian, I should think. He looked round him at the German people in the room. They still seemed unsuspicious. He fell to thinking of the prison camp – wondering what they were doing now – until John roused him and they went out to buy their tickets for the train.

Once again Peter stood back from the queue while John bought the tickets. Peter joined him as he left the queue. They went upstairs and across a footbridge, without speaking, and came to the barrier at the end of the platform. John handed the tickets to the collector.

The collector handed the tickets back and said something Peter did not understand. John replied in German. The collector shouted and pointed first to the tickets and then to the destination board which read KÜSTRIN. John blushed and looked at the tickets. He turned away, and led Peter to a quiet place away from the people who were crowding the platform.

'What's the matter?' Peter whispered.

'They gave us tickets to Berlin instead of Küstrin. It sounds much the same in German. I'll go and change them.'

'No – it'll need too much explanation. Keep them and go to another grille and buy two more. We've plenty of money.'

John looked relieved. 'O.K. I was wondering how to cope with the explanation.'

They went back to the booking hall and bought two

more tickets, this time to Küstrin. They got past the ticket collector who was now shouting at someone else; and on to the platform.

'Get into a crowded compartment,' Peter said, and climbed into a third-class compartment more like a cattle truck than a passenger coach. He entered through the door at the end of the coach. It was a non-smoking section and separated from the rest of the coach by sliding doors. Through the glass of the sliding doors he could see that the other part of the coach was overcrowded.

'We'll stay here,' he said. 'Perhaps no one else will get in.'

They sat there until the sliding doors were opened by a German soldier. He shouted loudly and began to push them out of the compartment. If only they wouldn't scream so much I might be able to get what they're talking about, John thought. He scrambled out of the coach and joined Peter, who was already on the platform. The man stood in the doorway shouting after them as they walked down the platform.

'What's wrong now?' Peter whispered.

John drew a deep breath. 'That carriage was reserved for Russian prisoners of war. I saw the notice on the side as we got off.'

'Definitely not the place for us!'

They climbed into another third-class carriage. This was full of civilians and they stood at one end of the compartment, trying to appear unconcerned.

The train stopped at every station and people got in and out. It seemed to Peter that the journey would never end. At every stop he expected the Gestapo to arrive, and stood in terror until the train began to move again. They did not talk. After a time they managed to get a seat and sat with closed eyes until they got to Küstrin.

They arrived at Küstrin at ten o'clock in the morning.

There was no identity card check at the barrier and they left the station and walked into the town. It was a small town, much smaller than Frankfurt, and Peter did not like the look of it.

'It's too small,' he said. 'We can't walk about here, we shall be noticed. Let's get out of the town and eat our lunch. There won't be any more workmen's trains until this evening and we can't hang about here until then.'

They left the station square and walked into the town. It was quiet, sleepy; and they were sure they would be noticed. After nearly two years of imprisonment the town was strange to Peter, frightening. He had not been in Germany before the war and he did not know what to expect.

They walked on down the main street of the town, past the thin queues outside the bakers' shops, until they came to a bridge over a canal. It was a hump-backed bridge and they could not see the other side. They had heard that bridges should be crossed on the right-hand side of the road and that all bridges were guarded. They did not know. Their only knowledge was from Kriegie gossip, from rumours and a smattering of information from prisoners who had been out before them.

'It's not worth it,' Peter said. 'It's not worth the risk. Fancy getting caught crossing a bridge. It's too true to form. Let's go back and try another road.'

They walked back into the town and took another road out. It led them to a public park.

'We'll eat here,' John said.

They rationed themselves to a cubic inch of the dog food and ate two of the American biscuits John had in his bag. When they had finished, John took out a clothes brush and they brushed their mackintoshes, their shoes and their hair.

'I shall have to shave soon,' Peter said.

135

'You look all right. Razor blades are scarce in Germany. Besides, you look more French like that.'

'I'm thirsty. We should have brought some water.'

'We'll go and get a glass of beer.'

'Oh, it's all right' – hastily – 'I'll carry on. We're all right as we are.'

'It's all right so far,' John said. 'We've been out seventeen hours now.'

'They don't know which way we went, that's one thing.'

'They're bound to inform all the railway stations.'

'Do you think we ought to walk from here?'

'I was just wondering.'

They sat in silence for a while.

'Look here,' John said, 'we're losing our grip. We said the open way was the best way and here we are skulking down side roads and talking of walking. Let's go into the town and have a beer.'

'Here comes a policeman,' Peter said.

John looked up. A policeman was walking slowly towards them down the path.

'That settles it. Let's go and have that beer!'

Without appearing to hurry they got to their feet and walked towards the policeman.

'Say something in French just as we pass him,' Peter said. 'Say something intelligent in case he speaks French.'

When they were within a few paces of the policeman John broke into voluble French. Peter tried to look as if he understood. And then they were past. John went on talking and Peter listened for the policeman to turn round; listened for the hail and the sound of pursuing footsteps. But he didn't turn round and they walked on like that for a hundred yards.

'What did you say?' Peter asked.

'I couldn't think what to say, so I told you all about a letter I'd had from my Aunt Annette who had bronchitis, and said that my sister Marie was having another baby.'

'Good show! It worked anyway. What shall we do now?'

'Go into town and have that beer. They serve a coupon-free meal in some of these places.'

'Yes, I know, it's called a *Stammgericht*.'

They found a café, went in and sat down. It was a large room with heavy, dark wooden tables and chairs. There were four men sitting at a table in the window. They looked like local tradesmen.

Peter and John sat at a table at the other side of the room. It had a red and white check tablecloth and a menu in a wooden holder. A waitress came from a room at the end of the café and stood by their table.

'*Zwei Glas dunkle Bier, bitte,*' John said.

'*Zwei Glas dunkles,*' she repeated, and went away. She returned shortly with two glasses of beer. It was dark beer in tall glasses, and each glass had a white collar of foam.

'*Danke schön.*' John handed her a coin. She groped in the pocket of her apron and handed him several smaller coins which he returned to her.

'*Danke sehr,*' she said, and smiled.

John lifted his glass and winked at Peter. 'Not bad, what?' he said when the waitress was out of earshot.

'Not bad.' Peter was watching the men in the window. They had stopped talking and were all staring.

Wonder what we've done wrong, he thought. Wonder if foreigners are allowed in here. Wish I knew more about it. It's all this working in the dark. We don't even know if there *are* such things as free French workers. It would be bad enough if we knew what to expect, but working in the dark like this we might barge into anything. Wonder if we can smoke in here. He looked again at the men in the window. One of them was smoking a pipe. He took out his cigarettes and offered them to John, who thanked him in French.

The waitress came in carrying a tray loaded with four

137

large white pottery bowls. They were steaming. She put one in front of each of the men. Peter watched closely. Money passed, but no coupons. This was the coupon-free meal. As she turned away from the table Peter caught her eye. He beckoned and gestured towards the table in front of him. She smiled and vanished into the kitchen.

The *Stammgericht* was a stew made from swedes, potatoes and carrots, but no meat. It was a generous helping, filling and warm. They had two more of the weak German beers and felt more full than they had felt since they had escaped. With a full stomach came renewed confidence.

'What do we do now?' John asked.

'Better not stay here. It'll look obvious if we stay here too long. Let's walk round the town.'

But it was worse in the street. Everyone seems to have something to do except us, Peter thought. Bad enough trying to spend an afternoon in a small English town, but this is getting on my nerves. This is going to be the worst part of the whole show, this trying to look inconspicuous with nothing to do. They tried looking into shop windows; but all the time the feeling of being watched grew more acute.

'I hate this town,' John said. 'Let's get out of it.'

'No – we mustn't catch a train until it's dark. We've got to stay here until it's dark.'

'We've got to do something. These one-street towns give me the willies. What about going back to the park?'

'Better not do that – we're inviting conversation if we sit there. Besides, it's afternoon now and all the women will be there. Much better to stay here.'

'I can't stay here,' John said. 'It's getting on my nerves. We're too conspicuous walking up and down the street.'

'Let's look at this objectively,' Peter said. 'What should we do in England if we had a few hours to waste?'

'Go to the public library or a museum.'

'Or to the cinema. Why not go to the cinema?'

John grinned. 'We escape from a prison camp and the first afternoon out we go to the pictures.'

'It'll be safer than the streets,' Peter said.

'I bet we're the first escaped Kriegies to go to the pictures.'

'That's why we'll get through. Keep it fluid. Do the natural thing. What could be more natural than going to the cinema?'

They walked towards the cinema, feeling better now that they were doing something, and less conspicuous. There was a queue, and they joined it. The queue was mostly children, with a few women, an old man and some soldiers. They were the only young men in civilian clothes. They stood at the end of the queue hoping that no one would talk to them.

It was not a comfortable cinema and most of the seats were broken. Peter found himself next to a young soldier who sat sleeping, his head fallen forward on his chest. He remembered the cinema in Cambridge. Of how he would go there in the afternoon when he had been flying the night before, and of how empty it would be up there in the balcony with only the chattering of the children in the pit below. Of the soft lighting and the organ music, and of how he himself used to fall asleep as soon as the lights went down and the picture started. Of how the sound of a shot or the sudden scream of the heroine would jerk him into wakefulness, only to fall asleep again to wake finally with a dry mouth and stagger out into the strong afternoon sunshine. And thinking of this he fell asleep until John wakened him when it was time to go for the train to Stettin.

It was nearly dark when they came out of the cinema and they walked quickly to the railway station at the far end of the town.

'What was the film about?' Peter asked.

'Oh, it was an escapist sort of film – a comedy about a Berlin family on holiday in the Alps. There was nothing about the war in it. I saw you were asleep and was rather frightened you'd wake up suddenly and say something in English.'

'I was too tired for that – slept like a log. I feel much better now.'

'I could do with a spot of the old bed,' John said. 'Didn't sleep much last night. I'd like to get my clothes off too. I'm sticky. I'd give anything for a bath and a good night's sleep.'

It was a small railway station and John felt conspicuous as he asked for the tickets. Stettin was a Baltic port, a more dangerous destination to ask for. The clerk demanded his papers. He produced his Ausweis and waited nervously.

'Your permission to travel?'

John handed over the rest of his forged papers. He tried to imagine he was buying a ticket in England.

The clerk picked up the papers and glanced at them casually. '*Gut!*' He handed over the tickets.

John took the tickets and his papers and walked away from the ticket office. He could hardly believe it. It had been as easy as that. He joined Peter and they walked up the steps to the platform.

The train was full and again they had to stand in the corridor. There were lights on in the corridor, which was so packed that it would have been impossible for a ticket collector to move down it.

It was a strain to stand there, surrounded by Germans, doing nothing, frightened all the time that they were about to be discovered. It was in the trains, when they could neither move nor speak, that they had time to think.

An hour later they stopped at a large station. Most of the passengers left the train here and a number of them went to the buffet where Peter could see them drinking soup. They were hungry and thirsty, but they stayed in the darkness of the railway carriage rather than brave the lights of the buffet.

When the train started again it was less crowded. They were able to sit on their bags in the corridor; and before long they were both asleep.

They were awakened by the sound of shouting. The typical bullying shouts of a German who has been given authority. It was the ticket collector, and with him were two of the Bahnhofs Polizei, the railway police.

John got the tickets ready and watched them work their way down the corridor, inspecting tickets as they came. In most cases the ticket collector merely said '*Weiter!*' as he handed the tickets back to the passengers, but occasionally he asked for their identity papers which were examined by the police.

Here we go, Peter thought. He glanced at John who sat white-faced and silent at his side. Next to him sat an old woman. As the men approached she showed obvious signs of panic. By the time the collector reached her she was almost crying with fear.

'*Ausweis, bitte!*' the ticket collector shouted.

The old woman fumbled in her bag. The ticket collector stood waiting. She produced a grimy piece of paper. The man handed it back angrily and shouted again. She said nothing but continued to offer the grimy piece of paper.

'*Polizeiliche!*' the collector screamed. '*Polizeiliche!*'

The old woman did not reply. One of the Polizei shook her roughly by the arm. The ticket collector grew red in the face. '*Polizeiliche!*' he shouted.

The old woman said nothing but sat hopeless on her bag. The collector said something to one of the policemen who took the old woman roughly by the arm and began to push her down the corridor. Peter could hear her whimpered protests as she was roughly jostled down the corridor towards the guard's van at the rear of the train.

The ticket collector turned to John, who handed over their tickets and waited apprehensively for the demand for their papers. The collector glanced at the tickets and handed them back without speaking.

When they had gone Peter sat on his bag in the corridor and broke out in a cold sweat. His knees fluttered and he felt sick. They had passed the first train check. The old woman had saved them. Their papers had taken them past the clerks in the booking offices but so far they had not been inspected by the police. He prayed that their luck would hold.

Just before eight o'clock the train began to slow down. Peter, who was dozing, was awakened by the changing tempo of the rhythm of the wheels. He looked at his watch and wakened John, who was sleeping on his bag in the corner of the corridor.

'We're running in, John. If the train stops outside the station let's get off. There aren't enough passengers aboard to make a crowd. I think it would be safer to jump off outside the station and walk into the town.'

'We'll be O.K.'

'We might need a special pass to go as far north as this.'

'You need a special pass to go anywhere,' John told him. 'We'll be all right.'

'If the train slows down we ought to jump.' Peter did not like this confidence in John. It had been easy enough in the camp to talk of travelling openly, but now he was frightened of it.

John got to his feet and dusted his trousers. 'O.K. – as you like. That was a pretty good sleep. I feel better now. What about a spot to eat?'

'We'll go into the lavatory and make some porridge.'

In the lavatory at the end of the corridor Peter opened

142

his case and took out a linen bag of dry oatmeal and a small tin. He mixed the oatmeal with water from the tap and handed the tin to John. 'I hope the water's all right,' he said. 'We should have brought some purifying tablets.'

'There's a lot of things we should have brought. We'll get by. It's a cinch now. We've done half the journey.'

'In terms of miles.'

John was feeling happy now and full of confidence. 'Let's go right in.'

'Not if the train stops. If the train stops we get out.'

But the train did not stop and before long they steamed into Stettin station.

There were more people on the train than Peter had thought, and they were swept towards the barrier by the crowd. John pushed forward to see if there was a paper check. He looked back at Peter and grinned. The passengers were handing in their tickets and passing off the platform without showing their papers. Then they were at the barrier. A quick tightening of the stomach muscles as they came under the lamp – a moment's panic – and they were through the barrier and free to go into the town.

Chapter Three

Nearly Caught

When they came out of the railway station it was raining. A cold wind blew in from across the Baltic bringing with it a fine, steady rain that whipped their faces as they stood in the bomb-damaged station square.

'We've got to find shelter of some sort.' John buttoned the collar of his mackintosh. 'Let's try the hotels. We'd better get in somewhere before midnight. There may be a curfew for foreigners in this town.'

'It's Saturday night.' Peter was still doubtful about the hotels. 'We haven't much hope of getting in.'

'We'll have to try,' John said. 'Unless we stay in the waiting-room until morning.'

'No fear! Waiting-rooms are the most dangerous places. Police check every two or three hours. Why not sleep out again?'

'It's too wet,' John said. 'Besides, we must find somewhere to shave. Come on!'

They stepped out into the driving rain.

Peter shivered. 'It's cold.'

'Walk fast,' John said. 'We'll soon get warm.'

They walked quickly down the street, past the shells of bombed buildings, gaunt and forbidding in the darkness. There were piles of rubble in the streets and the pavements were uneven and broken where the bombs had fallen.

'Pretty good mess, what?' Peter said. 'I wonder if any hotels are still standing. We could sleep in one of these bombed-out houses.'

'Too risky. They might think we were looting. Get shot for that in Germany.'

The streets were dark and strangely quiet.

'I hope there isn't a curfew,' Peter said.

'We'll know when we try the first hotel. Even if there is we can explain that we've just come off the train – though I can't see what reason we can give for getting off here instead of going straight on to Anklam.'

'You say that as it's Sunday tomorrow we thought the factory would be closed. And we thought it would be better to stay for the weekend and go on up to Anklam on Monday morning.'

'I doubt if I could say all that in German.'

They walked on down the dark wind- and rain-swept street, peering into each doorway as they passed.

144

'It's this infernal blackout,' John said. 'It's worse than London.'

'I wonder what Phil's doing,' Peter said.

'If he hasn't been caught he'll be in Danzig by now – he'd have arrived in Danzig last night. He's either on a boat or in a police cell by now.'

'He wasn't equipped for sleeping out.'

'No, he won't sleep out. His was an "all or nothing" effort. He's either on a boat or back in the cells.'

Peter laughed. 'I bet he's sitting in the hold of some ship eating margarine samples and wondering about us. I don't think he gave very much for our chances.'

'That's why he didn't come with us.'

'I'm glad he didn't,' Peter said. 'Three would have been too many. He binds too much. He'd have been binding all the time because it's raining. Remember how he used to bind all the time when we didn't dig because of the rain?'

'We must have been pretty trying,' John said.

They stopped outside an imposing stone building with a classical portico and mahogany revolving doors.

'It looks like a club.' Peter was doubtful. 'It doesn't say it's an hotel.'

'Perhaps they don't in Germany. We might as well try anyway.'

John pushed his way through the revolving doors. Peter followed, feeling suddenly disreputable and ashamed of his appearance. The carpets were too deep, the air of solid German respectability too strong. He caught John by the arm.

'Let's get out of this,' he whispered.

He moved quickly towards the swing doors. John, infected by the sudden panic in Peter's voice, moved with him. They passed quickly through the swing doors and out into the darkness of the street.

'What's the matter?' John asked.

'I don't know. I don't like it. Let's try somewhere else.'

'What was wrong with it?' John said.

'I don't know – it seemed wrong somehow. It didn't seem the sort of place foreign workers would stay at. Let's try somewhere else.'

'We can't walk round all night looking for hotels.'

'All right, we'll try the next one. But I've got a hunch about this place.'

'You're always getting hunches – and I'd got my German all ready.'

They walked on down the street until they came to a smaller building with a dimly illuminated sign which read 'HOTEL'.

'That looks all right,' Peter said.

John walked in and Peter followed. The lobby had linoleum on the floor and smelled of disinfectant. In one corner was a box for the night porter. The box was empty. In the opposite corner the linoleum-covered stairs rose crookedly to the floor above.

They stood waiting in the middle of the lobby. The place was silent.

'I'll go upstairs,' John said.

Peter followed him, not wanting to stay alone in the hall. Not wanting to be left to cope with his lack of German without John. On the floor above was a landing. Opening off the landing were several doors. One was open. There were beds in the room, beds standing in rows, and orderly, as in a barrack room.

'This is no good,' Peter said.

He led John quickly down the stairs and out on to the street. They were in the street again and it was still raining. John was growing angry.

'What the . . .' he began, but Peter went on down the street.

'That was too cheap,' he said. 'It was a sort of doss-house.'

146

'What if it was? It's a bed and it's dry.'

'They're likely to ask questions in a place like that. It's too cheap. They're likely to have police checks and goodness knows what. It's the sort of place they look for deserters in. We want a more expensive place.' He was shivering.

'You said that last place was too expensive. We can't afford to be choosy.'

'We've *got* to be choosy. That's just what we've got to be. If the place is too cheap it's dangerous because it's liable to police checks – and if it's too luxurious it's dangerous because we're conspicuous. We've got to find a quiet, respectable family hotel.'

'Then we'd better ask a policeman,' John said angrily.

'We might do worse than that.'

'Don't be silly!'

They were both angry now. Angry and tired, frightened and wet to the skin. Angry and bewildered because they hadn't imagined it would be like this; angry because they were suddenly without a plan and outside the routine they had known so long.

Presently they were at the bottom of the hill, walking along the main street towards the centre of the town. They had tried several hotels, but they were all full.

'It's no good,' John said at length. 'It's Saturday night. Let's walk out of the town and find somewhere to sleep.'

'O.K.' Peter said it with relief. 'We'll find a hotel tomorrow,' he added. 'We'll find somewhere dry to kip down tonight. A railway arch or something.'

'Which way shall we go?'

'Let's go south. If we go north it's the sea, and east and west we go along the coast.'

He took the small compass from his pocket and studied it by the light of his torch.

'We'll go down to the Square,' he said, 'and take the main road going south.'

They walked down a long, straight, concrete road with a cemetery on one side and large brick buildings on the other.

'If the worse comes to the worst we can sleep in the cemetery,' John said.

'It'll be locked. They always lock cemeteries at night.'

'We can climb over.'

'It's not worth it. We might be seen climbing over. It's not worth the risk. I don't suppose it would be very comfortable anyway.'

'No, but it would be quiet.'

They walked on past the cemetery, past the large buildings, until they came to an area of small suburban houses.

'This looks like going on for miles,' John said.

'I wish we knew if there was a curfew.'

'Even if there is, I don't expect it's until midnight. What time is it now?'

Peter looked at his watch. 'Eleven-thirty.'

'Well, we've got half an hour before midnight. We'll push on and see what we come to.'

And all this time they were walking down the long, straight, concrete road, with the rain slanting down, running down inside their collars, soaking their trouser legs, falling, bouncing back off the pavement, steady, continuous, drumming rain.

When they had been walking for some time Peter saw a policeman approaching them, tall, jack-booted and wearing a sword.

He was on the opposite side of the road, but when he saw them he started to cross.

'I'll talk French,' John said. 'Be listening to me, but look at him as you go past.'

148

'Let's run.'

'No – look at him. We'll be all right.' He began talking fast in French.

They went on as they were. The policeman crossed the road to intercept them. He's going to stop us, Peter thought. What shall we tell him? What excuse can we give for walking out here at this time of night?

'Tell him we're going to visit friends,' he whispered, but John went on talking in French.

They were abreast of the policeman now and Peter looked at him. He half stopped as though to accost them, and John let fly a torrent of excited French. He waved his hands and hunched his shoulders. He's wonderful, Peter thought. What a man! Good old John. And they were safely past the policeman and he hadn't stopped them. But he had stopped. Peter could not hear his footsteps and imagined him standing there watching them and wondering whether to turn and follow.

'Turn down here,' he said.

It was a side street. They turned down out of the policeman's sight. Peter quickened his pace.

'I think he's following,' he said. 'I don't think he likes the look of us.'

They were at the end of the street. It was a cul-de-sac and there was no way out.

'We've had it now!' John said.

'Through the garden – quick!'

Peter glanced over his shoulder. The policeman was standing at the top of the road watching them.

'Look as though we're going into the house.' Peter walked into one of the front gardens where he was hidden from the policeman's sight.

'He's coming down the road,' John said.

Peter tried the gate leading to the back garden. It was locked.

'Give me a hand.'

John stooped and locked his hands. Peter put a foot in them and caught the top of the gate. He hauled himself up and put down a hand for John. Then they were standing, trembling, on the far side of the gate.

'We can't go back,' John said.

'Let's climb over the fences into the next street.'

'O.K., but look out for dogs.'

There was a low fence at the end of the garden. They climbed it and found themselves ankle deep in newly turned earth.

'It's allotments,' John said.

'Find a path and cut along behind the houses.'

They found a path and followed it along the fence. It was dark and quiet and slippery, and there seemed no way out.

'We'd better sleep here,' Peter said.

'What? Among the cabbages?'

'No – in one of these air raid shelters.' He had stopped behind one of the gardens and pointed to a covered trench near the fence. 'Let's crawl in there and sleep.'

'It'll be dry at least,' John said. 'I'm wet through.'

They climbed the fence again and crawled into the air raid shelter. It was a trench. W in plan and about four feet deep. It was so built that it was difficult to lie down and impossible to stand up. The rain had seeped in and formed a thick slime of mud on the bottom of the trench.

'A typical goon effort,' John said.

'Uncomfortable – but I expect it's safe enough.'

'I don't only want safety. I want sleep. Let's go and find a more comfortable one.'

They tried several and finally found a wooden shed with earth banked up at the sides and the top covered with turf. Inside was a bale of straw. As an air raid shelter it was useless. As a hideout for the night it was just what they were looking for. They took off their mackintoshes and their boots and socks.

150

'I could do with a drink!' Peter said.

'Put out the old tin and collect some rain-water.'

'I will. I'll put it out now and then we'll have a drink for tomorrow morning.' He rummaged in his bag for the tin. 'What about a spot of porridge?'

'It'll take too long to collect the water. I'll have a piece of dog food. What I want most is sleep.'

Peter took out the dog food and cut two pieces about two inches square. He cut it by the light of the torch shielded in John's hands. The air raid shelter looked warm and comfortable in the dim light. 'We could live here for days,' he said.

'We've got to have a base in town. This is too far out. We must get somewhere where we can wash and shave, otherwise we'll begin to look like tramps. Respectability's the thing. My jacket's soaked. Are you taking yours off or leaving it on?'

'I'm leaving mine on – it'll dry quicker like that. We'll burrow down in the straw and they'll dry on us.'

'I hope we wake before it's light. Don't forget we've got to get out of this place.'

'The policeman will be gone by then,' Peter said. 'We'll wake up all right. I give us about three hours and then we'll be awake shivering.'

'Not me!' John said. 'I'm really sleeping tonight.'

He burrowed down into the straw and Peter heaped more on top of him. Presently they were both asleep.

Chapter Four

The Chase In The Docks

When Peter awoke it was still dark. At the moment of waking he thought he was back in his bunk in the prison camp and he put up his hand to rearrange the rolled-up shirt under his head. Then he felt the straw, and he was fully awake and remembering where he was. He fumbled in his jacket pocket for the torch and, shielding the light under the jacket, he looked at his watch. It was five forty-five. He flashed the torch over John. He was sleeping like a child, one hand under his head and his hair falling forward over his face.

Peter rose quietly and opened the door of the air raid shelter. It had stopped raining and there was a keen wind. He looked up at the sky. It was paling slightly in the east and scattered remnants of cumulus cloud chased one another across the horizon. A few stars showed in the full zenith of the sky and the air smelt good and clean.

Well, this is our second free dawn, he thought. He looked carefully all round him – at the backs of the houses and then at the allotments behind. Not a light showed. In the distance he could hear a faint clanking of a shunting train and suddenly close at hand a cock crowed loudly. It's Sunday morning, he thought, perhaps people won't be getting up so early. We'd better get moving though. We must find somewhere to get a shave. And then a meal.

He stooped to where he had left the tin. It was half-full of water. He went back into the shelter and mixed some dry oatmeal with the water in the tin. He shook John gently by the arm.

'*On appel, mein Herr,*' he said. '*On appel, bitte, mein Herr!*'

John grunted and rolled over.

'Come on, wake up, John!'

John opened his eyes.

'Come on, John, time to get cracking. I've made some porridge.'

John grunted again. He ran his fingers through his hair and groaned. 'I've got a mouth like the bottom of a parrot's cage.'

'It's a lovely morning. Eat some porridge and we'll get out of here before anyone else is about.'

'I'm stiff!' John said. 'I can hardly move. I think I've got rheumatism.'

'Nonsense – you've been sleeping too heavily, that's all. Here's your breakfast. Leave half for me.'

John began to eat slowly. 'I'm hungry enough, but this stuff takes some getting down.'

'You'll be all right once you get it inside you,' Peter assured him.

John ate half the porridge and handed the tin to Peter. 'Is that all we get?'

'I've got some biscuits but I thought I'd save them until we can get a drink.'

John put on his collar and tie and then his socks and shoes. He got to his feet and stumbled towards the door. Peter collected his things together and joined him outside in the garden.

'Shall we go back the same way?' John asked.

'I was just thinking. There must be a way out other than through the garden. We don't want to be seen climbing over the gate. Let's walk down behind the houses.'

They walked back along the path behind the fence at

153

the bottom of the gardens until they came to an alleyway between two of the houses. This led them out on to the main road.

'If we don't find anywhere we'll come back here to-night,' Peter said.

'We shan't need anywhere,' John told him. 'We'll get a ship. This is going to be our lucky day.'

The sun was shining as they came into the city and the streets were clean and sparkling in the freshness of the morning. Early workers were hurrying to and fro and the first tramcars were grinding their way up the steep hills of the town.

'Where do we go from here?' John asked.

'Let's go down to the docks and have a look at the shipping.'

They walked down the steep cobbled street until they came to the docks. There was a sea breeze and the air was full of the sea. There were ships in the harbour, some of them wearing their wartime coat of grey paint, others painted black and red and white, brave and toylike in the sun. As Peter and John drew nearer they could see that most of them were flying the German flag.

They did a quick tour of the docks, walking fast to avoid suspicion, but they saw no neutral shipping. Most of the bigger ships lay moored away from the quayside. The smaller boats were berthed alongside the quays but these were obviously fishing vessels and no use to them.

'This isn't what I expected,' Peter said. 'I expected to find them at the side of the docks.' He realised then that he had not really thought of the escape beyond the railway. He had always thought of the docks as being the objective. Getting to the docks had been as good as getting home to him. Now they were there, and the difficulties were just beginning. From now on they would have to make their plans as they went along.

154

'They've got to load and unload sometime,' John told him.

'Perhaps the best thing would be to hang around a bit and see what happens.'

'Better not hang around the docks too long. That's just where they'd expect to find us. Let's take a walk round the town and get the lie of the land. We'll try a few more hotels and get a room for a couple of nights. What we want is a headquarters. Then we can take our time and make our plans.'

They walked up into the town, this time through the shopping centre, with the shops shut because it was Sunday and the streets crowded with people. It was strange to be free to walk through the streets again. To look into shop windows and see the cars and motor buses with their wood burners attached to the luggage carrier or towed behind on two-wheeled trailers. It was strange to be among people who had a purpose in life, who had somewhere to go, who were not just passing the time until the next roll-call or waiting for the soup to arrive.

Three hours later they again found themselves down by the docks. All this time they had been searching for a place to stay. Everywhere they had been told that the hotel was full.

'This is a dead loss,' John said. 'I feel inclined to stow away on one of these fishing boats and trust to luck.'

'We mustn't be in too much of a hurry,' Peter told him. 'It's taken us four and a half months to get as far as this. We don't want to throw it all away in a few minutes and get marched back to the camp after being out for a couple of days. This is all new to us and it's worth giving it some thought. We must get out a plan of campaign. Here we are in Stettin and we want to get to Sweden. We've a little German money, good papers – we've proved that –

155

and fairly good civilian clothes. We speak a little German and we have some food.'

'Yes,' John said, 'and we've nowhere to sleep tonight and there's most likely a curfew for foreign workers. We've got to be safely stowed away somewhere by the evening. Most of the ships in the docks seem to be German. Even if they were Swedish, I don't see how we could get out to them.'

'The only way is to meet the sailors ashore,' Peter said. 'Contact the crew ashore and arrange with them to get us on the ship.' It seemed simple to him as he said it, merely a matter of speaking a few words and perhaps the exchange of a little money.

But John was reluctant. He wanted to keep the thing as small as possible. To talk to complete strangers was making the thing too big – spreading the risk. 'I don't like to,' he said.

'But you said yourself we can't just wander aimlessly around. We've worked to a plan so far and now we've got as far as we planned.'

'O.K. – we'll see what we can do. But if we have no luck by the afternoon we must organize somewhere to sleep before it gets too late. We don't want to get picked up on the streets after the curfew.'

'Come on, snap out of it – we'll be all right.'

Peter had been holding back because he was without a plan. But now he could see it clearly – to meet some of the seamen ashore. To make their arrangements to stow away safely – away from the docks. Not to go dashing into things, but to work slowly towards their objective.

They walked along the quays, looking at the men now and not at the shipping. There were Polish workers with the large 'P' on a brassard worn on the arm, Ukrainians and Lithuanians with 'OST' stencilled on their clothes, and scores of Frenchmen wearing an odd assortment of military uniform. In addition to these – all of whom were prisoners working under armed guard – there were the seamen of all the occupied nations, some in civilian clothes and some in the uniforms of their companies.

As they walked along one of the quays they came to a group of haggard men, stooping, thin and weary, with their feet tied in rags and tattered remnants of green uniform hanging from their backs. By their queer spiked cloth helmets and ragged appearance Peter knew them to be Russians. These men were barely alive, too weak almost to lift the picks and shovels with which they were supposed to work. They moved slowly, eking out their meagre strength, never smiling, doomed to slavery until the war was over.

So long as they kept on the move and were not obviously loitering they felt safe enough in this polyglot crowd and moved slowly among them, trying to learn as much as they could about the docks.

'If we get caught again,' John said, 'we could try to pass as Frenchmen. If we get returned to this sort of thing it won't be so bad. Far better than being in a British camp. Look at the chance these chaps have of getting away.'

'Let's have a word with one of them,' Peter said.

'I've told you before, I don't like to talk to them. They'll know I'm not one of them by my accent, and it's dangerous.'

'We shan't get anywhere unless we take some sort of risk,' Peter said. 'We've got to speak to them sometime.'

'Yes – but not in the docks.'

'The docks are as safe as anywhere else if you get them alone. Pick one that's walking on his own and ask him.'

'Ask him what?'

'Just speak to him in French and ask if he can tell you where to stay for the night.'

'Supposing he starts to yell.'

'He won't yell. We'll go down some dark side street off the docks and stop one there and ask him.'

'All right,' John said. 'But I don't like it.'

'I don't like it either, but we've got to take the risk sometime.'

'All right, I'll try. You stand behind him while I'm talking and if he yells sock him behind the ear.'

'I'll sock him behind the ear all right. I'll clock him with the tin of dog food.'

They went down one of the quiet roads leading off the docks and accosted some of the more obvious Frenchmen who came along. In every case the man looked at them nervously and hurried on without speaking.

'What's the matter?' Peter asked.

'They know I'm not a Frenchman. I expect they think I'm a German – a sort of "agent provocateur". This seems to be hopeless. I wish I knew exactly what these fellows are. They're French all right, but they don't seem to be prisoners of war.'

'Let's try this one.' Peter indicated a short, olive-complexioned man of about thirty years of age walking slowly towards them down the street. He wore a beret like themselves and a leather jerkin. Round his neck was a brightly coloured handkerchief.

'He's the last one,' John said. 'I'm frightened of some of the others coming back with the Gestapo.'

He spoke to the Frenchman. Peter stood on one side, ready to go to his assistance if necessary. There was a quick exchange of fast-sounding French and the French-man pointed down the road. He appeared to be giving minute instructions with many extravagant gestures and emphasis, and finally shook John warmly by the hand. John said something to him and the Frenchman looked at Peter, smiled and called, 'Salut!'

Peter grinned, wondering what it was all about. The Frenchman again shook hands with John, slapped him on the back, waved to Peter and walked on down the road.

'What did he say?' Peter asked.

'I think he guessed what we are. I didn't tell him, but I think he knew. He gave me an address – the Hotel Schobel. He advised me not to stay there more than two days, because, if you do, they have to send your papers in to the police.'

'Where is it?'

'Down by the docks. It's not a very posh place, but he says that they usually have some rooms free.'

'O.K.,' Peter said, 'let's go there.'

They found the Hotel Schobel in a road leading off one of the docks. It was a large building, old-fashioned and shabby. The entrance hall had a tiled floor and a lavish display of carved woodwork and uncleaned brass.

They were greeted by the proprietor, a stout German with a close-cropped bullet head and half-spectacles, smoking a large curved pipe; a German of the last generation.

John began his carefully rehearsed German. '*Haben Sie ein Doppel-Zimmer . . .?*'

Yes, apparently the proprietor had a double room. He pulled a bunch of blue forms from a drawer in his desk and handed them to John.

Peter pressed forward to see what John was writing. To his surprise the forms were printed in German, French and English. They filled in two of the forms, taking care to print in the continental manner they had practised in the camp. MARCEL LEVASSEUR, Peter wrote, BORN LILLE, 17 JULY 1914, EMPLOYED BY METALHUTTENWERK DR. HOFFMAN & CO., BRESLAU. NORMALLY RESIDENT IN LILLE.

John wrote, MARCEL, CONDE, BORN PARIS, 2 OCTOBER 1921, EMPLOYED BY METALHUTTENWERK, BRESLAU. NORMALLY RESIDENT IN PARIS.

They produced their Ausweis to prove this and were asked to show their police permission to be in that town. John showed the form giving them permission to travel to Anklam and explained that they wanted to stay in Stettin for two nights so as to arrive in Anklam on Tuesday morning. The proprietor asked for his money in advance. And then they were free to go to their room.

It was a large room, the walls covered with floral wallpaper. A wardrobe stood against the wall opposite the door and a grotesque dressing-table filled the space in front of the single window. There was a double bed surmounted by floral drapes and a tiled stove like the outside of a public house. In one corner, incongruously, stood a white washbasin with chromium-plated hot and cold taps.

'Well, here we are,' John said. 'The first thing I'm going to do is wash.'

He took off his clothes and crossed to the washbasin. From ankles to wrists his body was black from the dye off the combinations he had worn in the tunnel. He turned on the hot water tap.

'It's a snare and a delusion,' he said.'

'What is?' Peter was unfastening his bag.

'This basin. The hot water doesn't work.'

'There's a war on, you know. I don't suppose they've got any coal.'

'Oh, well, we'll have to manage in cold.'

He took a piece of Red Cross soap from his bag and began to wash. Peter lay on the bed watching him.

'Why do you think those forms were printed in French and English?' Peter asked.

'Oh, they had them before the war, I expect, and they're still using them.'

'No wonder the Germans have an inferiority complex. Just imagine if English hotels had registration cards printed in German.'

'They wouldn't have. English is an international language.'

'Our menus are printed in French.'

'Yes, but that's to kid ourselves. Not to help foreigners. That's just to kid ourselves that the cooking's good.'

'What couldn't I do to a Chateaubriand steak!' Peter said. He lay on his back on the bed as he had so often done in the prison camp, conjuring up his ideal meal. 'A Chateaubriand steak garni, with spinach and French mustard, followed by green figs in syrup.'

'Oh shut up!' John said. 'Make some porridge.'

'Or a grilled Dover sole swimming in butter. Or even a good mixed grill.'

'Shut up!' John was standing on his towel furiously scrubbing at his legs. He looked very young standing there, thin and young and graceful against the background of floral wallpaper.

And suddenly Peter realized that John was near to breaking point. That talking to these Frenchmen had taken the last of his nervous strength. He cursed himself for a selfish fool. He had been pushing John harder than he should. 'You don't want any more porridge,' he said. 'We'll get washed and go out and get a couple of beers and a Stammgericht.'

'O.K. – but don't talk about food. I feel as though I haven't eaten for years.'

'You've hardly eaten for forty-eight hours. I had a meal just before I left. I've got a spot of chocolate – how about that?'

'Yes, please,' John said, and ate it there and then standing on his towel by the washbasin.

While John finished washing Peter slit open the lining of his mackintosh and took a waterproof bag from under the armpit. He opened it and took out a map which he spread out on the bed. With the map were a Swedish sailor's identity card and some German money.

'It's the Freihafen we want,' he said, studying the map. 'If we cross over the second bridge from the railway station it'll bring us straight to it. That's where the Swedish ships will be – if there are any. The dock we were in this morning was all wrong. If we get no joy at the Freihafen we'll go on to Reiherwerder coaling station and see if there's any chance of stowing away on a coaling barge.'

'Is the club marked on the map?'

'Yes – Number Seventeen Kleine Oder Strasse. But we won't use that except as a last resort. Remember what Stafford said. It's too dangerous.'

The Freihafen was protected by an eighteen-foot diamond mesh wire fence with three strands of barbed wire running along the top. There were arc lamps over the wire and armed guards at the gates. The place looked like a prison camp.

They walked slowly round the outside of the docks. There were wooden buildings inside the wire but between them they could see the hulls and the funnels of the ships.

Suddenly John caught Peter by the arm.

'Look – a Swedish ship!' Peter could see the black hull of a ship with the yellow cross and *Sverige* painted on her side.

'We'll get on board tonight,' John said. 'We'll come back after dark and climb aboard.'

'There's bound to be a watchman on board,' Peter said.

'It'll be one of the crew. They wouldn't have a German watchman in a guarded dock.'

'I don't like it,' Peter said. 'I'd much rather try and get hold of one of the crew ashore. It's sticking our necks out to go into a place like that.'

'We wouldn't be here if we hadn't stuck our necks out. Besides we can't speak any Swedish and if we've got to talk to the crew it's going to be much safer in

162

the ship than out here surrounded by goons. Anyway, she might be gone by tomorrow.'

Peter allowed himself to be persuaded. He still did not like the idea of climbing into the docks, but as John said, they had to take some risks. By avoiding all unnecessary risks they might remain free, but they would not be getting anywhere.

They made a careful inspection of the fence and chose a spot where a railway siding ran close to the wire. It was halfway between the two arc lamps and by climbing on to the truck which stood on the siding they would be able to reach the top of the fence.

'Now we've got to find an exit,' Peter said. 'We may want to come back.'

They chose a shed standing near the wire. It was directly in the light of the arc lamps but it was the only means of getting out of the docks.

They spent the afternoon at the cinema. The film was a story of ancient Germany called *Paracelsus* and to Peter, whose lack of German made it difficult for him to follow, it was not exciting. He sat there dreading the evening. Dreading the risk of climbing into the guarded docks, but seeing John's point of view. Seeing that unless they took the risk they would never get out of Germany.

They came out of the cinema and went straight down to the docks. There was a sentry patrolling the railway siding outside the wire. They walked down the road past the siding and stood, apparently in conversation, watching the sentry. He was doing a steady beat up and down the siding, his rifle slung from his left shoulder.

'Next time he turns his back we'll slip in behind the truck,' John said, 'and climb on top. We'll wait for him to come up again and then next time he turns away we'll nip smartly down into the docks.'

'We'll go and have a look at the place where we're

163

going to climb out first,' Peter said. 'If there's a sentry there we'll call it off. We may want to come out in a hurry.'

They walked round the outside of the fence to the shed but they could see no more German soldiers.

'It's O.K.,' John said. 'He's guarding the railway siding, not the dock.'

Peter felt committed; but he said nothing.

They climbed the fence carefully, one at a time, taking their feet slowly from the wire to stop it twanging. The fence was slack and when they reached the top it swayed so that the one who stood on the ground had to hold it still for the other. The noise of the climbing ran along the fence and they were frightened that the sentry would hear.

Peter had been dreading this the whole afternoon. But once he was over the fence and inside the dock and creeping in the darkness towards the quay where they had seen the Swedish ship, he felt a completeness that he had rarely felt before. An aloneness, an awareness of himself as a vulnerable entity, a feeling that came only when he was hunted. It was not only the danger of the thing. He had not felt like this when, as a member of an air crew, he had been stalked by night fighters. It was more animal than that. It was nearer to the earth. And as he crept forward in the darkness towards the black bulking outline of the shipping in the docks, he felt a thrill of pleasure in the game that he was playing and an added awareness of the clean air blowing in from the sea.

When they reached the quay the Swedish ship had gone. At first they thought they had come to the wrong quay and they cast round looking for her. They took a bearing on a large German vessel they had seen from the road and realized that they were in the right quay; but the ship had sailed.

It was dark in the docks and they had to use a torch to read the names on the counters of the ships. They had explored two of the quays and were about to move on to a third when they saw a light jerking towards them across the open ground at the end of the quay.

Peter saw it first. 'Look out, we've been seen!' And he ran towards the sea end of the quay.

There was a whistle and shouting, and lights flashed out in front of them from the end of the quay. He caught John's arm and turned sharply to the right between two warehouses and out on to the other side of the quay where they crouched behind some barrels. He was panting now and wishing they had never come into the docks. John lay beside him, panting too. And then they heard the sudden yelping of the dogs.

We've had it now! Peter thought.

John gripped him by the arm and nodded away towards their left. A German soldier with a storm lantern was passing them, walking towards the sea end of the quay.

'That's the light we saw.'

'Let's cut away towards the left – towards where we came in.'

They came out from behind the barrels and crept down the side of the warehouse towards the main part of the docks. Suddenly there was a guttural '*Halt!*' behind them. They started running together, running fast, expecting all the time to hear the rifle crack and feel the impact of the bullet in their backs. There were more shouts now and the dogs yelped again.

They were running side by side and running hard, making for the open part of the docks, away from the confinement of the quays. They came round the corner of the warehouse going fast and crossed over some railway lines.

Peter was panting in earnest now. There was a pain in his side and the air felt like cold water as it went down into his lungs.

Then John was in front, running easily. He turned sharply to the left into a dark alley between two of the warehouses. They came to a concrete railway platform raised some eighteen inches above the level of the ground. John dived under it and Peter followed, full length on the dry earth under the concrete and panting, panting so that he felt his chest would burst. They lay there panting and spent, drawing the cold burning air into their lungs and expelling it quickly to snatch more.

They lay for some time listening to the sound of the German soldiers searching the docks. Several times they heard voices loudly at the end of the alley where the platform was. But the searchers did not go down and the sound of voices grew fainter and finally ceased altogether.

They lay under the platform for an hour and a half before they considered it safe to come out. Then they came out from under the platform and stood listening. They were cold now that the sweat had dried on them and stiff from lying on the cold ground.

'Let's make our way towards the fence,' Peter suggested. 'We'll follow the railway down. There's bound to be a gate where it enters the docks.'

They followed the railway, walking now. Walking softly on the sleepers and slowing down as they came to a branch in the line. There was an arc lamp over the points, but they did not see the sentry until they were right on top of him. Then they stopped dead. He was standing just to one side of the railway line, looking at them as they came down the line.

'Walk on,' John whispered, and walked on down the line, ignoring the sentry.

'*Halt!*'

They stopped and the sentry came towards them.

'*Ausweis, bitte.*'

They took out their wallets and handed him the papers. He looked at them. Studying them closely as a man will who does not read easily. He was middle-aged and looked stupid. As they stood there Peter could smell the German soldier smell. The smell of ersatz soap and German tobacco. The smell of German sausage and sauerkraut. The man put the papers back into the wallets, creasing them with his thick fingers as he pushed them in. Hope to God he doesn't ask for our dock passes, Peter thought. But the sentry, apparently satisfied, handed back their wallets. He said something in German and John replied.

'*Ach so?*' said the sentry, and laughed.

And then they were past him and walking on down the railway line.

'What did he say?' Peter asked.

'He was suspicious at first. He asked what all the shouting was about and I told him someone had fallen in the sea and they were trying to get him out. Then he seemed amused – perhaps it was my accent. I think we'd better get out of here.'

'It was a darn' sight easier getting into this place than it's going to be getting out,' Peter said. 'I bet they've got guards posted outside by now.'

'I don't think so – it doesn't mean that they thought we were escaped prisoners. They may have thought we were Frenchmen doing a spot of pilfering. If they've scared us off I expect that's all they worry about.'

'I hope you're right.'

They went on down the railway line until they came to the fence. Everything was quiet now. But they were not taking any chances. They lay listening for ten minutes before Peter spoke.

'Creep up to the fence and when I say "Go" we'll both climb up together. If we're seen, go like blazes when you get to the other side and I'll see you back in the hotel.'

They crept quietly up to the fence.

'O.K.?'

'Yes.'

'Go!'

They covered the short distance to the fence in a few paces and began to climb. Climbing quickly and as silently as possible. Expecting every minute to hear shots from the guards inside the wire. But the shots did not come and they got safely down on the other side and ran two blocks before they felt it was safe enough to stop and talk.

'So much for the docks!' Peter said.

'We were just unlucky.'

'Unlucky be damned! We were lucky not to be shot. We were lucky enough to get out of there without being caught.'

Chapter Five

The French Workers

Peter awoke to see John standing fully dressed by the washbasin. He was wearing Peter's blue mackintosh and a beret pulled down over his eyes.

'Where are you going?' Peter asked.

'I'm not – I've been.'

'Where?'

'Down to the docks.'

'What on earth for?'

'I thought I'd go and have a look round.'

'Then you're a fool. Supposing you'd got caught. I shouldn't have known where you were.'

'I left a note for you,' John said mildly.

'Why didn't you wake me up and tell me you were going?'

'I woke up and couldn't get to sleep again. You were sleeping pretty soundly and I didn't want to wake you. I lay there thinking for a bit and decided that the best time to contact the Frenchmen was in the early morning, just as they were going to work, before it was light.'

'Why didn't you wake me? I'd have come with you.'

'Well – as a matter of fact,' John looked embarrassed, 'I thought perhaps I'd have more success if I went alone. I lay in bed wondering why they all seemed so scared when I spoke to them and I came to the conclusion that (a) the Air Force mackintosh I was wearing looked too much like the German "Feld grau," and (b) the fact that you were hanging around in the background made them suspicious. So I thought I'd just go down in your mackintosh and put it to the test.'

'I think you might have told me. I'd have worried if I'd known. Did you have any luck?'

'I'll just get back into bed and then I'll tell you all about it.'

John undressed again and got into bed beside Peter.

'It's too cold out. I'm not getting up again until ten o'clock.'

'What happened?'

'Well, it was just as I thought. I got down to the French camp in the docks just as they were all streaming out to go to work. I tagged on to a chap who was all alone and walked down the road with him. I didn't tell him I was English, just said "Good morning" and walked along beside him. I asked him where the Swedish boats were berthed and he confirmed that it *is* the Freihafen. I asked him where the Swedish sailors go in the evening

169

and he said either the club in Kleine Oder Strasse or the cafés down Grosse Lastadie Strasse. He didn't think there were any neutral ships in the Freihafen at the moment. You need a dock pass to get into the Freihafen. He showed it to me – it's on a pink card.'

'Does he work in the docks?'

'They all work in the docks in that camp. They unload the ships.'

'What did he say about the curfew?'

'There's no curfew for foreigners in this town. But all the French workers who live in the camp have to be in by ten o'clock.'

'Did he give you any suggestions?'

'No, he wasn't a bit helpful really. He answered the questions I put to him, but that's all. When I didn't ask him questions there were awkward silences. These chaps don't speak my sort of French. I had to repeat each question about six times and even then I'm not sure I understood the answer. But there's a chap in their camp who speaks English. He said if we go along there tonight he'll have him there to meet us.'

'Now we're getting somewhere! What time?'

'He said to go along any time after eight o'clock. He showed me where the hut is. We're to climb in over the back fence.'

'Do you mean we're to climb into the camp?'

'Yes.'

'Well I'm darned! We nearly got shot climbing into the docks last night – now you want to go climbing into a prison camp.'

'It's the safest place to talk,' John said. 'Safer than talking in a café.'

'You said that about the docks.'

They both lay silent for a while, warm and comfortable in the large bed, secure behind the shut window, listening to the noise of the traffic in the street below.

'Is it very closely guarded?'

John smiled. 'They're not guarded at all. There's an old civilian gatekeeper who books them in and out of the camp, but apart from that they can come and go as they please.'

'We'll go along tonight and have a look at it,' Peter said. 'Let's get up now and go and find that coaling station at Reiherwerder. There might not be a fence round that.'

Reiherwerder coaling station lay about four kilometres outside the dock area and according to the map could be reached by tramcar. They followed the tram track out. There were docks and coaling stations all along that road, approached by narrow lanes running off the main road. At the entrance to each lane was a swing gate and a watchman's hut.

It was a grey morning and they walked quickly to keep warm. There was little traffic, but they passed several foreign workers with the yellow letter 'P' on a diamond-shaped patch sewn on to their jackets. There were girls too, heavy peasant girls, in wooden clogs and blue overalls with the word 'OST' printed on them in yellow letters. They were laughing as they walked, in scattered groups, towards the coal yards.

'I don't like the look of this,' Peter said. 'I don't think we'll get much joy here.'

'We'll push on,' John said, 'we'll see what it's like at Reiherwerder.'

Half a mile up the road they were stopped by a level crossing. A long train of empty coal trucks was steaming slowly into the docks.

'That's the way to get in!' John said. 'Come up here after dark and jump one of these trains. It'll take us right into the coaling station.'

Peter did not reply, while they waited for the train

171

to pass. He was afraid of John's impetuosity. To jump a coal train. To leave the safe guise of a French worker and become an escaping prisoner. To be committed. To go in with no way out. To take the final step that might lose the whole game. They were safe now, part of the crowd. To jump a train would be to break away from the crowd, become conspicuous.

The train clanked slowly by.

It would be too easy. Stretch out a hand, a quick jump and you were in. But once in, you were committed. Someone might see you. You had made the move that would commit you for the rest of your time. It wasn't worth it.

'Look here, John, let's not rush our fences. We're quite safe as long as we take things quietly. We could live here for weeks – as long as the money lasts.'

'That's all very well, but we're not getting anywhere. There's no point in just living here. The object of the exercise is to get to Sweden.'

'I couldn't agree with you more. Surely our best plan is to talk to some more Frenchmen and find out more about these places before we start climbing into them.'

'And tell half Stettin what we're doing! That's a risk, if you like. I think it's risky talking to anyone.'

'Not as risky as climbing into places. Just suppose we were French workers, as we pretend to be. Even then we'd be breaking the law by going into the coaling station. By not breaking any laws we could stay here as long as we like.'

'Yes, but where's it getting us?'

'Nowhere at the moment, I admit. But we've only been here a day and I don't think we should go charging into things. After all, we've got plenty of money and time's no object.'

'Then what have we come to Reiherwerder for, anyway?'

'Now you're just being silly.'

'I'm not being silly. We decide not to use the Freihafen again, so we come out here. We find a good way of getting in here, and you want to cry off.'

'I don't want to cry off. I just want to be certain about it.'

'How can you be certain about it – how can you be certain about anything here?'

'We can be more certain after talking to the French. After all, they've been here longer than we have. We wouldn't have found a hotel if it hadn't been for a Frenchman.'

'That's true. We were lucky that time. He might just as easily have given us away.'

'That's true, too.'

'Then what are we arguing about?'

'I don't know. Let's push on to Reiherwerder.' Peter suddenly realized that they had been arguing heatedly in English, their voices rising as their tempers rose. His last words had been spoken as the clanking of the train died away in the distance, and the high English words rang across the street.

'Come on, John,' he muttered in a low voice. 'Sorry if I lost my temper.'

Before they came to Reiherwerder they had to cross a bridge. On the far side was a barrier guarded by a German soldier. They stood for some time watching people crossing the bridge.

'It's all baloney about crossing bridges on the right-hand side,' Peter said. 'They cross on both sides.'

'Yes – what's more, if you go across in a tram you get over without having to show your papers.'

'You'd have to show them to the conductor when you buy your ticket,' Peter said. 'It's not worth it. Let's go back and try a few cafés in the town. Then this evening we'll go and have a look at that French camp. Look – there's a Frenchman over there. Go and have a natter to him.'

'You're always wanting me to natter to Frenchmen. What do you want me to ask him?'

'I'd do it myself if I could, but you know I can't speak French.' Peter felt the helplessness of his position. 'Ask him if he knows where we can find some Swedish sailors.'

They crossed the road and John spoke to the Frenchman. Peter listened, not understanding. Then a tram came along and the Frenchman got on to it. Peter moved after him but John held him back.

'What did he say?'

'He spoke a sort of argot I couldn't understand. Perhaps my French isn't as good as I thought it was. Either he didn't understand me or he was too scared to talk. I didn't want to get on the same tram in case he wanted to carry on the conversation in front of the Germans.'

'Never mind. We'll go back into the town on the next tram and go round a few of the cafés. When it's dark we'll have a look at the French camp.'

They spent the afternoon exploring the cafés round the docks. Frightened to stay too long in any one place, they went from café to café, having one drink in each and passing on to the next. Everywhere they felt conspicuous, felt all the time that people were watching them, that their clothing was not right, that they were doing something which made them stand out from the other customers.

As it grew dark it became more difficult. They could not see inside the cafés before they entered. After stumbling into one full of German soldiers they decided that it was time to go to the French camp.

It had been easy getting into the camp. They had no

difficulty in finding the hut and now they were standing in a room full of Frenchmen and smelling again the odour of captivity.

There was a silence when they came into the room. A sudden silence and then a resuming of the conversation in a lower key. A closer drawing-together of the men round the table and some laughter and loud remarks from the men on the bunks against the wall.

John's contact of the morning was there. When he saw them he rose to his feet, mumbled a few words and went out through a door at the back of the room.

'Where's he gone?' Peter asked.

'To fetch the chap who speaks English, I expect.'

Peter looked round him at the familiar scene. The room was very like the one they had lived in. Here, perhaps, the smell was stronger than he had known it – that unmistakable, unforgettable, compounded prison smell. The room was dirtier and showed less ingenuity and improvisation; but it was the same room, the same bunks, the same wooden clogs under the bunks.

But the men in the room were not the same. Peter felt the resentment all around him. He did not feel among friends. The Frenchmen were eating and as they ate they watched. A dozen pairs of eyes watched them as they stood by the stove waiting for the contact to return.

'I wish that chap would hurry up,' Peter said.

'Not a very promising bunch, are they?'

So they stood, simulating indifference until the English-speaking Frenchman came to take them to his room.

The men in this room were more polite. They stood when John and Peter entered and offered them coffee and black German bread. Peter in return produced a packet of French cigarettes.

The English-speaking Frenchman was halfway through his meal and excused himself in broken English, explaining that he was the camp barber and had to cut hair after

175

the others returned from their work. He was a thin, sharp-featured man of about thirty-five. He looked cleaner than the others and wore a collar and tie.

The barber's English was not as good as the contact had led them to suppose. When Peter asked him in English about the Swedish ships and sailors he did not understand and John had to ask most of the questions in French. While they were speaking in English the other Frenchmen were silent; but when John spoke in French they all replied together at such a speed that Peter found it difficult to follow.

The French were apparently delighted that the English prisoners had escaped. For the escape they offered their felicitations and their admiration. But as for helping them – it was too bad. They would have liked to help – but the Germans. They would be shot if they were caught. It was too bad.

When John asked the barber about the Swedish ships and whether he could make a contact for them among the Swedish sailors, he replied that he himself did not work in the docks. But he had friends in the docks and he would find out from them. He sounded confident, but he also made it sound too simple. The whole time they were talking there was an atmosphere of fear. It seemed to Peter that the French were anxious to get rid of them. That their presence was an embarrassment and a danger.

They finally gave it up as hopeless. The more they talked the less promising it seemed to be. They traded cigarettes for black German bread and asked the barber to tell all the other French workers that there were two escaped English prisoners in Stettin and that they could be approached through him. They offered a reward to anyone who would help them.

They got safely out of the camp and walked back towards the town.

'So much for the French,' Peter said. 'They're a dead loss.'

'Oh, give 'em a chance,' John said. 'At least we know we can get bread for cigarettes now. And if they tell the others we may find someone who's got the guts to help us.'

'They certainly didn't seem too keen. They're not even guarded.'

'They couldn't go anywhere if they did escape,' John said. 'Not much point in going back to France. Besides, they've been subject to German propaganda for years now.'

'They've got their beer and cigarettes. They're just sitting pretty waiting for the war to end.'

'There are bound to be some good types,' John said. 'I expect they're all in the underground movement and lying low. They'll make contact when they get to hear about us.'

Chapter Six

Things Get Complicated

John lay in bed watching Peter shaving in front of the mirror over the washbasin. He finished shaving and began to wash himself all over with a face cloth he had cut from the tail of his shirt.

'What's the programme for today?' John said.

'We'd better go and have another look round the docks, I suppose.'

'I thought you decided against climbing into the docks.'

'I don't mean climb in – I mean mark down a few

177

cafés for this evening. You can't see what you're doing in the dark.'

'Are we going to start all that café-stalking again?'

'It's the only thing to do, John. We made one contact last night but that's not enough. We've got to get every Frenchman in the town working for us.'

'I don't like it,' John said.

'It's safe enough. We won't tell 'em where we live. We'll just make a rendezvous like you did with the last chap. We're bound to strike oil sooner or later.'

'Better make it sooner then. The money won't last for ever. We've got to move out of this hotel today. We can't go on like this.'

'Shall we go back to the air raid shelter?'

John pulled the sheet up round his ears. 'We'll find another hotel all right. We've got enough money for three or four more days. What have we got for breakfast?'

'I've got enough porridge for one more meal. And there's the bread we got from the French last night.'

'Let's go down and have breakfast in the hotel.'

'Too risky. No sense in running into trouble.'

'Come on, Pete – a hot drink will do us good.'

'It's not worth risking it for a cup of coffee.'

'Come on, Pete – we'll take down some of the bread and eat it with the coffee. Start the day with something warm inside us. Things will look entirely different after a cup of coffee.'

'We'll go and see what it's like. If there are many people there it won't be worth risking.'

When John was ready they went down to the dining-room on the ground floor. There was an empty table with a banquette seat in the corner. They sat on the seat with their backs against the wall. A waitress came over to them and John ordered coffee. She brought a pot of coffee and two cups. John poured the coffee and they knew at once by the smell that it was made from acorns.

John took the bread from the side pocket of his coat. It was wrapped in a copy of the *Völkischer Beobachter*. Peter looked round quickly to see if they were being watched. There was an old lady at the next table and on the far side of the room an elderly couple were studying the morning paper. In the middle of the room a middle-aged man who looked like a commercial traveller was writing in an exercise book. Except for the heavy smell of German cigarettes and an occasional '*Heil Hitler!*' from the foyer they might have been in some provincial hotel in England.

They sat there eating the bread and drinking the ersatz coffee. Peter relaxed and sat back on the seat. They were fooling them all along the line. He glanced casually towards the door and stiffened suddenly as he saw the German military uniforms in the foyer.

There was no other door out of the room. What he had always feared was to be in a room with only one door. He had dreamed of it in the camp. A room with only one door, and the Germans there.

The two German officer gave a perfunctory '*Heil Hitler!*' as they entered the room. They made straight for the table where Peter and John were sitting. As they approached Peter felt his stomach contract and the piece of bread he was eating stuck in his throat. Always that sudden contraction of the stomach and the desire to run. The exhilaration came afterwards. First the blind, unreasoning panic to get away. Only after that came the exhilaration and the trembling at the knees.

But the two officers were not looking for them. They were an oberst and a major and both carried black brief-cases. The major was wearing jackboots and spurs and had a scar from the left eye to the corner of his mouth. He carried an ornamental dagger from chains at his waist and on his collar he wore the red artillery flash. The oberst was more quietly dressed. He was in slacks and carried no dagger, but he wore the insignia of the Knight's Cross of the Iron Cross.

What do we do now? Peter thought. Do we stand up when they get here? Do we speak to them? Do we 'Heil Hitler'? Is it done for foreign workers to eat at the same table as German officers? And he went on eating his bread. There was nothing they could do. They could not walk out leaving their coffee and bread on the table. They just had to sit there and take it as it came and trust that their luck would hold.

The Germans sat down at the table. They both had thick colourless skin and closely cropped hair. Peter felt the revulsion that he always felt when he was close to a German officer. The oberst wore pale-blue spectacles and his mouth was small and tight. He ordered coffee and began to talk to the major.

Peter glanced at John out of the corner of his eye. He looks young, he thought, we're O.K, we'll be O.K. We'll just sit here for a minute and then we'll get up and walk out.

The major opened his briefcase and took out a bundle of papers. He put on a pair of rimless spectacle and began to explain the papers to the oberst. Listen, John, Peter thought, this may be important. He grinned inwardly. Don't be an ass. Colonels don't discuss military secrets in cafés in front of foreign workers.

They finished their coffee. John looked at Peter and raised his eyebrows. They rose without speaking and left the hotel.

'What were they talking about?' Peter said. 'Was it important? Could you get any of it?'

'I couldn't follow it very well. It was some educational scheme, I think. They were talking about the Hitler Jugend and the Hitler Mädchen.'

'Preparing for the next war, I expect,' Peter said.

They tried several dockside cafés that morning, including one that the French barber had told them was run by a Communist. This was a low, square room with a door opening directly on to the street. It was full of seamen and dockside workers who were sitting at round metal tables drinking dark beer out of tall glasses. In this café there were no pictures of the Führer, nor did the customers give the Nazi salute on entering and leaving.

They chose a table in a corner where they could talk without being overheard. In the more crowded cafés they could not talk in English. They had to sit in silence the whole time; and if they wanted to talk they had to go into the lavatory, and there was usually somebody in the lavatory. But in this café they could talk comfortably and they sat in the corner sipping their beer and watching the people at the other tables.

Peter sat watching the two Frenchmen who were sitting at a table in the opposite corner of the room. They were young and their dark hair and olive skins looked warm and vital compared to the Germans around them. They sat with their heads close together in argument. They look just like us, Peter thought. We must look exactly like that when we're whispering together. I wonder what they're talking about. The more he watched the more suspicious the two French boys seemed. They each had a bundle tied up in coloured cloth and the one facing the room cast nervous glances round him as he spoke.

'Just look at those two frogs behind you,' Peter said. 'Move over here so that you can see them without turning round.'

John moved over next to him. 'They do look a bit furtive, I think I'll saunter over and have a word with them.'

Peter watched him as he crossed the room. He's as young as they are, he thought, and looks as French.

John was standing by the table now, looking down. The

two Frenchmen had stopped talking and looked scared. He sat down with them at the table and Peter saw them grow less scared. He saw John pull his Kriegsgefangener identity disc from his pocket and show it to them across the table. I won't join them, he thought, I'll stay here and watch, and if they get too suspicious-looking I'll go and warn them.

But John refused to allow it to look like a conspiracy. He took out a packet of cigarettes and leaned back in his chair. He called a waiter, ordered more beer and then when he had finished he bade the Frenchmen farewell and rejoined Peter.

'I scared them out of their lives,' he said. 'They were planning to stow away in a Swedish ship and I went up and leered and asked them if they could put me in touch with any Swedish sailors. They thought I was a member of the Gestapo who was just playing with them before he ran them in. They were scared stiff.'

'I thought they looked pretty scared.'

'They were scared stiff. They live in a camp about ten miles outside Stettin and they come in as often as they can with all their luggage wrapped in a bundle, ready to stow away. They really thought they'd got it that time.'

'Were they any help?'

'Not really. They don't know any more about it than we do – rather less if anything. They've been trying to stow away for six months now. Money is their difficulty. They said a pal of theirs saved up forty marks, which was the price asked by a Swedish sailor, and the fellow took it and handed him over to the Germans.'

'What a dirty thing to do.'

'They know who he is and they say the next time he comes to Stettin he'll get a knife in his back – that's if he ever comes here again. He won't if he's got any sense.'

'Where do they try to stow away?'

'Reiherwerder. They've got passes. They know a chap

182

who works down there. Apparently they work alternate day and night shifts and when he's on nights he lets them have his pass during the day. They reckon they can stow away in a collier.'

'I wonder if we could get hold of one of the passes.'

'I've fixed that. They're going to bring a couple along tomorrow. We can't keep them for long, but I thought perhaps you could fake a couple of them up. They don't look very elaborate affairs.'

'I should be able to.' Peter was eager to take some of the work off John's shoulders. 'I brought some Indian ink with me and one of the rubber stamps. We should be able to fake something up all right.'

'Good show. I'll go down to the coaling station with one of the passes tomorrow afternoon while you make a couple of copies at the hotel.'

'If we've got a hotel by then.'

'We'll find one all right. We'll go and find one now. And then we'll go and make a few more contacts.'

They went to several more cafés before they booked a room. They were now living on two cups of acorn coffee for breakfast, vegetable stew at midday, and a square inch of dog food before they went to bed. On some days they had managed to buy another plate of stew or potato salad in the evening.

This was the fifth day of their freedom and they were running short of money and food. They had eaten the last of the oatmeal and were saving two of the tins of dog food to eat on board the ship. Although they wore warm clothing they were always cold; the cold came from inside, it was a coldness that only food would warm. The constant strain of living in the heart of an enemy city was beginning to tell on their nerves, nerves that had been almost at breaking point during the long anxious weeks before the tunnel broke. They found themselves arguing over the most obvious decisions. They had a long argument before deciding to spend their precious marks on the cinema. But it was warm in the cinema and they had not sufficient food to keep them warm. It was dark and in the darkness they felt safe. In the cinema they could relax and drop for a moment the constant guard upon their actions and their tongues. And they came out again rested and ready to start once more on their circuit of the cafés.

'We've got two tentacles out,' Peter said. 'The barber and the two boys. They cover two of the camps. What we want tonight is a chap from another camp. If we go on long enough we'll have our feelers out in every camp in Stettin.'

'It's too slow. Money's getting short and if I don't get a square meal soon I shall faint on you in the street. Where are we going to sleep tomorrow night? We haven't had much luck with our contacts so far.'

'We're doing pretty well, if you ask me. We're dry, clean and shaved – and we've still got some money left.'

'It won't last us long. If we don't strike oil soon we'd better get out of here and jump a goods train up to Danzig.'

They walked on for some time in silence.

'Let's go and have a look at that club,' John suggested.

'It wouldn't be open yet, would it?'

'I don't know. What time do these clubs usually open?'

'I don't know.'

There was a short silence.

'Where did you say it was?' John asked.

'Seventeen Kleine Oder Strasse.'

'Let's go and have a look at it.'

They walked down a steeply cobbled street on their right and came out on the Bollwerk. There was a watery moon rising above the river and the streets shone wetly where they were lit by the shaded street lamps. They followed the river for a hundred yards and then turned to the the left again. Kleine Oder Strasse lay on their right hand, a narrow winding alley cutting darkly between the houses. They followed the alley down until they came to Number Seventeen, a tall house without lights in the windows. On the right-hand side of the door was a notice which read, NUR FÜR AUSLÄNDER.

'Doesn't look very glamorous,' Peter said. 'You'd most likely have to show your papers as you go in. Doesn't it say "Foreigners Only" on that notice?'

'Yes.'

'It's too dangerous. We were told not to go there except in dire need. And you could hardly call this dire need. It's nearly a year since Stafford got that information about this place and the Gestapo are bound to have got on to it by now. They've probably got one of their own people in the place as a spy.'

John looked again at the face of the dark house with the abrupt and unequivocal sign.

'What about going in and having a look round?' he suggested.

'It's not worth it. You'd most likely have to show your papers as you went in.'

Once again they started on their round of the cafés. At the first three they drew a blank. In each case the French were too near the Germans. It would have been impossible to talk to them without being overheard.

They went back to the café where they had met the two French boys. It was still uncrowded and they sat where they had sat before facing the café and watching the seamen, dock-workers and unidentifiable Germans who seemed to stand on street corners all day wearing nautical caps and smoking pipes.

'Not a very promising bunch,' John said.

'That fellow looks all right.' Peter indicated a thin, wild-eyed Frenchman who was leaning forward haranguing the other men at his table. His eyes were alight with enthusiasm and he seemed to be urging them to do something against their will.

'Wait till he goes to the lavatory,' John said. 'I'll talk to him and you stand behind him in case he yells. He's the last one I'll try. If he's no good I'm finished for the night.'

'O.K. I'll fix him if he yells.'

But the man did not go to the lavatory. He looked at his watch, excused himself and made for the door.

'After him!' Peter said, and they left their beer on the table and followed him out on to the street.

They caught him in the street just before he turned the corner and Peter heard John say, '*Pardon, M'sieur, nous sommes prisonniers de guerre anglais . . .*' But the Frenchman took him by the arm and hurried him back into the café before he could say more.

Peter followed them in and they sat at the table where they had been sitting before. The Frenchman was pale and still gripped John by the arm. The men who had been sitting with him before he left the café turned and watched them as they sat down. The Frenchman spoke to John in a fast whisper.

Why must he look so furtive? Peter thought. Why does he have to make the whole thing look like a conspiracy?

'He wants to see your Kriegie disc,' John said.

Peter took the Kriegsgefangener identity disc from his pocket and handed it to the Frenchman, who took it and rubbed his hands together, the disc between his palms.

'*Mon Dieu, il fait froid! On gêle ce soir*,' he said, and shivered theatrically, cupping his hands and blowing into them, surreptitiously peering at the disc as he did so.

186

He'll get us all arrested if he goes on like this, Peter thought.

The Frenchman handed back the identity disc under the table, carefully looking round the room before he did so. By this time most of the customers were eyeing them with curiosity and Peter began to feel uncomfortable. The Frenchman was talking to John in a low voice, his mouth hidden behind his hand.

'He wants to take us to another café,' John said. 'He says he can put us in touch with some Swedish sailors there.'

'He'll put us all in jail if he's not careful. What does he want to act like that for?'

'He says he's a member of the Underground. But I can't understand half of what he says. He says that the café he wants to take us to is "sympathetic".'

'O.K.,' Peter said. 'Let's get out of here.'

Sympathetic, he thought, they're all sympathetic. Why can't they talk without looking furtive all the time? Those two boys looked furtive enough but this chap looks like a stage villain. Perhaps they always look like that. Perhaps it's me. Perhaps I'm getting nervy. Perhaps they don't look furtive at all. Or perhaps the Germans are used to it and don't notice it. Anyway, I don't like it, it frightens me.

When they came to the café the Frenchman led the way in and Peter and John followed. This was brighter than the other cafés and there were women. The Frenchman chose a corner seat and ordered beer. John tried to pay for it but the man pushed the money away. '*Gardez les sous,*' he said, and began to talk.

The French was too fast for Peter and he looked round the room. It was a cheerful place and there was some music. A seedy-looking young man in a stained dinner-suit was playing a piano. There were some German soldiers and they each had a girl. It was light and the people looked happier than they had in the other cafés. It smelled of food, good meat food, and there were tablecloths on the tables.

The door opened and four German soldiers came in. They looked enormous as they came in the door and Peter realized how difficult it would be to get out of the place. There was only one door and even if one soldier was standing there it would be impossible to get out. He looked round for the lavatory. It would be as well to have another exit. There was a door in the corner marked HERREN and he crossed over and went in. It was the usual affair with a small window opening on to a lane at the back of the café. He made certain that the window would open and went back to the table.

'There's a window in the bog,' he told John. 'If anything happens we can get out that way.'

'Good show.' John turned again to the Frenchman.

Peter leaned back in his chair. A woman sitting at the next table smiled at him. She had red hair and her smile was an invitation. He was alarmed. He leaned towards the other two, assuming an interest in their conversation. The Frenchman was about to leave. As they stood to shake hands a waitress passed their table. The Frenchman stopped her.

'My friends are Swedes,' he said in loud German. 'They are lonely in this town. If any Swedish sailors come in this evening show them to this table, please.' And then he left the café.

The fool! John turned to Peter, but it was too late. The red-headed woman was sitting at their table talking earnestly to him in a language that was neither French nor German. Peter sat there looking frightened, obviously wondering what to do. He played his trump card. He rose to his feet. '*Ich bin Ausländer,*' he said with dignity, '*nicht verstehen,*' and walked with determination towards the lavatory.

The woman turned to John, addressed him in the same language.

'I do not speak Swedish,' John said in German.

'But your friend said you were Swedes.'

'My friend you were speaking to is Swedish. I am French.'

'He did not sound Swedish,' the woman said.

'He is very drunk.'

The woman began a long apology for speaking to them without an introduction. She was heavily made up and was about to cry.

'My friend is not well,' John said. 'Please excuse me.'

When he got to the lavatory Peter had locked himself in. He knocked the 'V' sign with his knuckles and Peter opened up.

'How was my German?'

'Awful,' John said.

'She's German, isn't she?'

'Yes, but she speaks Swedish – I don't know how much, but she speaks it all right. She started off in Swedish, but I interrupted her and told her I was a Frenchman. I told her you were a Swede but you'd gone to the lavatory to be sick.'

'I've opened the window,' Peter said. 'Lock the door – we'd better get out of here.' He stood on the lavatory seat and thrust his head and shoulders through the window. John heard him grunting, then he wriggled back, red in the face. 'We'll have to go feet first,' he said. He swung on the water pipe and managed to get his legs out of the window. He landed with a thud in the street below.

John followed, giggling. 'I wonder what they'll do when they find the door locked.'

'Break it down, I expect. We won't go back to that place.'

'You can say that again,' John said.

189

Chapter Seven

The French Are Suspicious

They rose early the following morning and kept their appointment with the French boys who brought the two dock passes. They spent the rest of the morning in fruitless wandering round the dockside cafés. After the episode of the Swedish-speaking German woman they were more cautious in their attempts to make contact with the Swedes. The lack of food and constant strain were having their effect. They fluctuated between extremes of caution and recklessness and as their moods did not always coincide they spent most of the time urging one another in opposite directions.

When they had eaten their midday Stammgericht they managed to book a room for one night at the Hotel Sack. This time they explained that they were returning to Breslau from Anklam, and were accepted without question.

It was a modern hotel and steam-heated. After they had been shown to their room John took one of the passes they had borrowed from the French boys and set out for the coaling station. Peter stayed behind in the hotel bedroom to make copies of the other pass.

He locked the door and took a flat tin box from his travelling-bag. Inside the box were bottles of red, black and Indian ink, a camel-hair brush, a razor blade, two mapping pens, a small metal ruler and a stamp cut from a rubber heel.

He made a careful study of the pass. It was a piece of

thin pale pink cardboard about the size of a playing card. In the left-hand top corner was the photograph of the holder; it was roughly the same size as the photographs on their Swedish passes. To the right of the photograph was the superscription. Below these in black German-gothic lettering was the usual list. Name, age, sex, height, eyes, hair; followed by the signature of the Chief of Police. In the left-hand bottom corner was the well-known imprint of the swastika-carrying eagle. Peter noted with satisfaction that all the particulars had been filled in with pen and ink – he did not feel capable of reproducing typescript accurately. It was not the shaping of the letters but the intensity of the ink that he found difficult to reproduce. The only way was to trace it through carbon paper and he had forgotten to bring any.

He took a sheet of thick paper almost as stiff as the cardboard on which the pass was printed and cut two pieces of the right size. He cut them carefully with the razor blade and metal ruler on the mirror from the dressing-table; absorbed now in what he was doing and forgetting the ultimate aim of his work. He would be absorbed for the rest of the afternoon and would finish the job with aching eyes and stiff shoulders; but rested and in some way renewed by the intensity of his work. It had been the same in the prison camp when he had been painting scenery or a watercolour. Then he had realized suddenly that an afternoon had passed with him absorbed and unaware that it had gone.

He gave the two pieces of paper a wash of clear water and left them to soak. He mixed a thin solution of red ink and water in one of the tooth glasses and washed this on carefully; giving them three washes before he was satisfied that they were nearly enough the colour of the pass. He left them to dry, flat on the glass above the radiator.

While the pieces of paper were drying he took some

191

tracing paper and carefully traced out the spacing of the lettering on the pass. He did not trace the actual lettering; it was too small for that. He was experienced enough to reproduce the German print freehand and with enough accuracy for it to pass for the real thing at a quick glance.

When the two pieces of paper were perfectly dry he pricked out the tracing through the tracing paper and started on the lettering. He wrote slowly, taking only sufficient ink on the pen to draw one stroke, and writing with the paper resting on the sheet of glass so that there would be no indentation made by the nib and the ink would stand up proudly. It was careful, finicky work and he only stopped to turn on the electric light or refill his pipe.

When at last he leaned back, yawned and looked at his watch, it was nearly ten o'clock.

They were not a good job. They were not nearly up to the standard of their other papers. But they would do. He removed the two photographs from the Swedish sailors' passes and stuck them on to the new ones with paste made from dog food.

Then he lay on his bed and fell asleep.

When John left the hotel there was a fine drizzle of rain falling and he buttoned his mackintosh tightly round his neck. The cloth beret he was wearing gave no protection to his face and as he screwed his eyes against the driving rain he cursed the nation that had adopted such idiotic headgear. It was cold and he would rather have stayed with Peter in the warmth of the hotel bedroom. But he had to get to Reiherwerder and carry out his inspection before it grew too dark, so he thrust his hands into the pockets of his mackintosh and bowed his head before the rain.

As he walked down to the tram stop he realized why so many escaping prisoners seemed in a way relieved when

192

they were caught and brought back into the camp. None of them seemed to suffer deeply from the disappointment of being caught. And now, huddled in his thin mackintosh against the cold and driving rain, he thought of the warmth and companionship of their room in the camp.

Now he was alone, even away from Peter. He had been alone in the prison camp, in the cooler, but this was different. He felt vulnerable and slightly lightheaded as he walked down the rain-swept street; an exaggerated facet of that mood which had haunted him ever since they had crawled from the narrow tunnel into the lesser darkness of the forest – a feeling of unreality, of too-good-to-be-true. He felt like an exotic bird escaped from a gilded cage, prey to the hardier natives. My heart is like a singing bird. He pulled himself together, grinned. A turtle-dove – a turtle-dove in a turtle-neck sweater.

When he got down from the tram the rain had turned to snow, and warmly, in that short time between dusk and the official black-out, a light was shining from the porter's hut at the entrance to the coaling station. He showed his pass and the sentry let him through. He walked quickly through the gate, past the sudden glow of warmth and light from the porter's hut, into the desolation of the dock. There huge mounds of coal loomed on either side of him and as he came out on to the quay he saw the coal tips standing gauntly against the solidity of the sky.

There were no ships berthed alongside the quay, but a short distance away to his right he saw a group of prisoners wearing the long tunics and characteristic cloth helmets of the Russians. Near them stood the German sentry, his heavy-booted and long-skirted silhouette barely visible through the driving snow.

Not much future there. He turned to his left. He had his back to the wind now and could see more comfortably. Ahead of him was a large timber building and to one side of it the smoke-blackened funnel of a steamer.

He walked on down the quay and as he came to the small shed he saw that it was a kitchen. There was a straggling line of men at the open door, each man holding a mess tin in front of him. They were Russians, and in the fading light of the afternoon their faces looked thin and pinched, wolfish under the mangy fur and grotesque ear-flaps of their helmets. Very few of them had coats and some were without shoes. Their rag-bound feet seemed to melt into the mud and slush in which they stood. As he passed them he saw one of the Russians pour half of his portion of soup into his companion's cup. And he walked on towards the steamer at the quayside feeling a glow inside him, an echo of the warmth that had come to him from that line of tattered men.

When he reached the quayside he found that the ship was German. He decided that had she been Swedish he could have climbed aboard. He hung around for some time anxious to find out whether a sentry was posted in the docks. The prisoners had finished work now and the guards were marshalling them into lines to march them back to the huts. It was foolhardy to hang around any longer and he left the docks and caught a tram back into the town.

He made for the café where he had arranged to meet the Frenchman who had left them so abruptly at the mercy of the Swedish-speaking German woman. I'll tell him off for that, he thought. It's no good being sarcastic. I couldn't manage that in French. I'll tell him how dangerous it was. I'll tell him not to be so furtive too.

The Frenchman was sitting at a table near the door. When he saw John he motioned him to a table some distance away.

Here we go again, John thought. More games of hide-and-seek. He sat down and ordered a beer.

The Frenchman had half a glass of beer in front of

194

him and he was smoking a cigarette. He did even this furtively, drawing swiftly at the cigarette and glancing round the café between draws. He did not look at John but kept glancing towards the door. John lit a cigarette and sat waiting for some sign from the Frenchman. He was growing angry now. What the devil was the fellow playing at?

When the Frenchman got up and went out John followed him into the street. The Frenchman led him out on to the Bollwerk down the first turning on the left and up past the club in Kleine Oder Strasse. They turned to the left at the top of the hill and the Frenchman disappeared into a doorway at the end of the street. I wonder if he wants me to follow, John thought. I wonder if it's a trap. And then he laughed at himself. There would be no point in laying a trap. They could have picked him up at the last place if they'd wanted to. So he went in.

It was a 'Wirtshaus', very like an English pub. There was the same heavy wooden panelling and long mahogany counter with the etched mirror behind it. The Frenchman was sitting with three other men in the far corner of the room. He was sitting forward, talking in a low voice and casting sidelong glances round the room. I shan't stay here long, John thought, my nerves won't stand it. He joined the Frenchman at the table.

When the Frenchman had introduced him to the other men he began to make excuses. He explained they were members of a Communist group and were engaged on very dangerous work. He hinted at sabotage and mentioned that the Germans had placed a price on their heads.

'I could not speak to you in the café. We were being watched. We are safe here. The publican is a member of the Party.'

'Then you cannot help us,' John said.

The Frenchman shrugged his shoulders. 'We each have our job to do. Yours is to escape and return to England.

Mine –' He shrugged his shoulders again. 'But we have some money. Would you like some money?'

'We are short of money,' John said. 'We also have need of food. Food is of more importance to us than money. If you could give us some ration cards we should be grateful.'

'We cannot give you ration tickets. We live on the black market. But we can give you food.'

He called the Gastwirt and ordered sandwiches. When they arrived John split them in two and put half in his pocket.

'For your breakfast?' the Frenchman asked.

'For my friend.'

'Then we will repeat the order.'

While John was eating they discussed his plans. When they heard how he and Peter were living they suggested that it would be better for them to get into a French camp. They told him that it would be quite safe living in a French camp; but they did not offer to take him into theirs. They warned him against staying in a certain hotel where the proprietor spoke fluent French, and advised him that a café called the Café d'Accordion was the best place to contact Swedish sailors.

He left them as soon as he could and made his way to the Café d'Accordion. Entering through the low swinging doors, he stumbled down three steps and found himself in a long low room filled with tobacco smoke and the sound of talking. There was singing too, the first he had heard in any café in Germany, and in one corner a pianist was accompanying a hunchback in gipsy costume who played an accordion. Most of the conversation seemed to be in French, although occasionally he could pick out the sing-song tones of Scandinavia. Next to the piano a girl in a tight sweater and a black skirt was sitting on the knee of a man in a seaman's jersey. She had one bare arm round his neck and was drinking a glass of wine.

As John came into the room he realized the hunchback was playing 'J'Attendrai.' This isn't real, he thought, this is Hollywood. This is a scene in Montmartre. This is a film setting for *The Rat*.

He ordered a glass of wine, leaned with his back against the bar and looked at the people in the room.

'J'Attendrai.' . . . He thought of his room in Oxford and the houseboat on the Thames. The portable gramophone and a record of Jean Sablon's. That tune had so many memories for him. He thought of that long summer on the Thames. Of Janet and going ashore at Shepperton. Drinking beer at the Anchor when they were both learning to drink and didn't like it much. His brother home from Sandhurst; and drinking pints. Janet poling a punt under the green shade of the willows, the water dropping from the pole in a cascade of diamonds and himself lying in the punt and watching her. His mother making tea over the Primus stove. And, always, somewhere in the background, the gramophone playing 'J'Attendrai.'

Then he saw the English-speaking barber. He was sitting at the back of the room behind a table full of glasses of beer.

He saw John and beckoned him across to the table. John took his wine over and sat with them.

'At last I have found you,' the barber said. 'This is Pierre. We have searched the town for you.'

'Have you heard of a ship?' John said.

'This is Pierre,' the barber said. 'I think that he will help you.'

John shook hands with Pierre; noticing how, as always before, the French were known only by their first names. Nor did they ask him for his name or any proof of his identity.

Pierre said, 'I have a friend who is going to Sweden in a Danish boat. He leaves tomorrow. I do not know how he is going or why. When I heard from our friend here

197

that there were two English prisoners in Stettin trying to get out of Germany, I approached my friend and asked him for his help. If you will come with me now you can meet him and perhaps he will help you.'

'Where is he?' John asked.

'I will take you to him.'

'Is it far from here?'

He shrugged his shoulders. 'Not far. But I will take you there.'

'I should like to tell my friend where I am going.'

'I am afraid that is not possible.'

'Very well. I will go with you.'

'Good,' Pierre said. 'That way is better. Do not walk with me but follow close behind. I will take you to my friend.'

It was a typical prison camp hut and it smelled strongly of French tobacco. The walls were covered with pictures torn from magazines and on one of the walls were painted the words VIVE DE GAULLE.

'Rest here,' Pierre said, and went out through a door at the back of the hut.

John sat on one of the wooden stools and wondered what would happen next. The man had led him by devious routes but he guessed that he was in the camp they had visited two nights ago.

A short while later Pierre returned, accompanied by two other men. They were big men and one of them was armed with a thick stick. The man with the stick stood by the door.

'What is your name?' the other asked in French.

'John Clinton. I am a British Officer.'

'He looks like a stool pigeon,' the man with the stick said. 'He has the accent of a Boche.'

'It might also be the accent of an Englishman,' the first one said. 'André will be here in a minute. He will know.'

There was a short silence.

'He has the look of a Frenchman,' the man with the stick said.

'You cannot tell by appearances, Raoul. All men look alike these days.'

'He is certainly not French.' This was Pierre, who till then had been silent.

'Of course I'm not French,' John said. 'I told you, I'm British.'

'We have to prove that,' Raoul told him. 'Do you know what will happen if we find that you are not British?'

'I tell you I *am* British!'

The man shut one eye and drew a forefinger across his throat. 'You will be found floating in the dock. No one will know how you came there. We had a stool pigeon before, did we not, Pierre?'

'André will know,' Pierre told him.

There was a long silence while John wished himself well out of this 'cloak-and-dagger' atmosphere. It was melodramatic, but it was also dangerous. Then footsteps were heard treading lightly on the path outside.

'Here is André,' Raoul said.

André's face was pale and his brown eyes burned darkly. He looked ill and walked with a stoop. As he entered the hut Pierre took him to one side and whispered in his ear.

He looked at John and came towards him across the room.

'Do you speak French?' He said it in broken English.

'A little.'

'Good. It is important that I speak fast. I leave for Sweden tomorrow. There is an organization. But first I must have proof of your identity.'

'I have my identity disc here.' John began to unfasten his coat.

'I regret that is not sufficient. What is your name?'

'John Clinton.'

'Your age?'

'Twenty-three.'

'Are you a soldier?'

'Yes.'

'What rank?'

'Captain.'

'What camp were you in?'

'Stalag-Luft Three.'

'What regiment were you in?'

'I cannot tell you that.'

'You do not trust me. It is right that you should not. But I must have proof of your identity. When did you escape from the camp?'

'Last Friday.'

'When were you captured?'

'December 17th, 1942.'

'Where?'

'Africa.'

'Were you in a tank?'

'No. I was on a motor cycle.'

'What make?'

'B.S.A.'

'Were you wounded?'

'In the arm.'

'Show me.'

John began to remove his coat.

'No. Do not show me. You look tired. Two years is a long time to be a prisoner of war.'

'I was only there for one year.'

'Of course.'

There was a silence. They stood facing one another. How can I help him, John thought. How can I prove that I'm what I say I am? It must be damn' difficult for them, but how can I trust them?

'What are your mother's Christian names?' André asked.

'Mary Elizabeth.'

'What does your father call her?'

'Betty.'

'Have you a garden?'

'Yes.'

'What flowers grow in it?'

'Roses, lupins, pansies, geraniums.'

'Have you a car?'

'Yes.'

'What make?'

'Morris.'

'Horsepower?'

'Ten.'

'Do you know London?'

'Fairly well.'

'What is the name of the statue in Piccadilly Circus?'

'Eros.'

'What is it famous for?'

'Its flower-sellers.'

'That is good. One more thing.' He suddenly slapped John lightly across the face.

'What the devil . . .!' John began.

All the Frenchmen laughed.

'I am sorry,' the man called André said. 'You have passed the test.' He turned to the short man. 'He is British all right. I, André, can vouch for that.'

'Good,' Pierre said. 'Now we can get down to business. First, you must eat.'

Chapter Eight

The Cafe d'Accordion

Peter was dreaming he had been caught in the tunnel. A fall of sand had pinned him to the floor and he was struggling to get free. It was dark and hot and the sand was smothering him. There was sand in his eyes, in his ears and in his nose. He was swallowing sand with every breath. And the more he struggled the more the sand kept pouring down from the roof. Someone was digging down to save him. It was John. He knew it was John and kept calling to tell him where he was. He could hear the thumping of the spade as John dug furiously away to save him before he suffocated. If only he could keep the sand away from his mouth he would be all right. He pushed his hands away from his face, clearing the sand away, pushing hard against the force of the onrushing sand . . .

Then he was in the hotel bedroom in Stettin. The sand was the pillow smothering his face and the weight of the sand was the weight of the heavy German quilt he had pulled over himself. The sound of John digging was a gentle thumping on the door. As he crossed the room to open the door he looked at his watch. It was ten-thirty.

'What did you lock the door for?' John asked. 'Afraid of the goons?'

'I locked it while I was working on the passes. I must have fallen asleep.'

'How did they go?'

'I don't know – haven't looked at them since I finished.' He crossed the room and picked up one of the passes. 'Not bad. Not bad at all, though I say it myself. What do you think?' He handed them to John.

'They're the right colour anyway. It's a pity we shan't have to use them.'

'Why? What happened? Come on – you're tired – sit down and tell me about it.' He dragged up the chair for John and sat himself on the bed. 'Now tell me about it.'

'Wait a minute. I've got something for you first.' John pulled out the now rather dirty sandwiches. 'Sorry I couldn't get any paper to wrap them in.'

'Where did you get these?' Peter asked through a mouthful of bread-and-sausage.

'That furtive chap gave them to me. He gave me some money too. Apparently he's a saboteur or some-thing and that accounts for all that "cloak-and-dagger" stuff.'

'They're good sandwiches anyway. Here, have one.'

'It's all right, I've had mine. I had a meal in a French camp too.' He told Peter everything that had happened since he had left the hotel.

'That Café d'Accordion sounds a pretty good joint,' Peter said.

'Yes – not bad. Beer's good too. Thought we might go there tomorrow night.'

'What about that chap Pierre? Won't he be looking out for us?'

'We can't depend on them,' John said. 'They talk so much. I rather think it's all talk. It's no use sitting back and depending on them.'

'Where shall we sleep tomorrow?'

'The Frenchmen told me to stay here, but I'd rather not. I don't altogether trust them. Besides, we only booked for one night and it would rouse suspicion to stay longer. Then there's the money question. What about trying another night in an air raid shelter?'

203

'I'm game,' Peter said. 'It can't be long now. We're bound to strike oil sooner or later.'

The following morning they stayed in bed as long as they dared. Now that they knew the French were helping them it was becoming more and more difficult to fill in the time. Every moment they spent on the streets was dangerous, yet they could not stay too long in the hotel for fear of arousing the suspicions of the proprietor.

They stayed in bed until lunchtime. It was raining again and they wanted to keep themselves dry for the night, when they might have to sleep in their clothes. Then they got up, had a bath in the washbasin and walked down to the Café d'Accordion. It was closed.

'Have they been shut down, d'you think?' John asked. 'It was a pretty blatant sort of joint.'

'Oh, I expect they only open in the evenings. Let's go and get a Stamm and come back later on.'

The café was crowded, but they managed to find a table for two. They had been eating in these places every day that they had been in Stettin and Peter was no longer dependent on John for his peace of mind. Now as always John did the talking and when he had ordered the beer and the Stammgericht he went to the lavatory to wash, leaving Peter to guard the table.

He had been sitting there for some time, day-dreaming. At first he did not realize that he was being addressed. Then he looked up and saw the angry German face glaring down at him. '*Ich bin Ausländer, nicht verstehen.*' He was about to say it when he realized that the German was asking him if the other chair was occupied. Nothing could have been more plain. The man was standing one hand resting on the back of the chair, his eyebrows raised in interrogation.

What shall I say? Pete thought. Where's John? The blighter will sit down if I don't say something. He smiled brightly. '*Das ist besetzt*,' pointing to John's chair; '*Das ist frei*,' pointing wildly across the café.

Then John came back.

'Some goon wanted your chair,' Peter said.

'How did you stave him off?'

'Oh, I explained that the chair was occupied and suggested that he sat somewhere else. He seemed quite a decent chap. Had quite a conversation with him as a matter of fact.'

After lunch they walked round the docks again. The docks they had come to know so well. Down the Bollwerk where the river Oder flowed dark and sluggish and the gulls wheeled and swooped in the sky, jeering and shrieking at them because they were earthbound and looking at them with yellow staring eyes as they swooped by in the perfect freedom of their flight. Past the motor torpedoboats, E-boats and ships' pinnaces lying waiting to dash out to the destroyers moored by Swinemünde. Past the Café d'Accordion still dark and closed, over the bridge and out opposite the gates of the Freihafen. There they found no neutral shipping and although they walked round several times they could not pick out the Swedish flag.

When it began to get dark they returned to the café where they had met the French boys. They sat quietly sipping their beer and watching the other people in the room.

Peter was thinking of the Frenchmen. Were they really any use? Was it worth the risk of hanging around or would it be better to make for Danzig? Phil had gone to Danzig and was probably in Sweden by now. They were getting too involved with the French. Perhaps John was right. Perhaps it would have been better to have kept it to themselves.

He found that he was looking at a man who sat at the next table. He had seen the face before. Noticed it several times, but almost subconsciously. It suddenly

205

seemed that the man had been in every café they had used. The face had cropped up time and again, but he had not consciously noticed it before.

It had caught up with them at last. It had been too good – too easy. Now that they were face to face with it he was almost relieved. It had been the uncertainty more than the danger that had got him down. He leaned over to John.

'See that fellow who's just come in?'

'Which one?'

'That one. Sitting near the radiator.'

'What about him?'

'He's following us.'

'Nonsense.'

'He is. He's been in nearly every café we've been in.'

'Why should he follow us? If they wanted to pick us up they'd do it without following us.'

'I don't know why,' Peter said. 'But he *is* following us.'

'Easily find out. Drink up and we'll go to another café.'

They finished their beer and without looking at the man they got up and left. They walked quickly down the street and went into another café. They ordered more beer and sat watching the door. The man did not come in.

'Imagination,' John said. 'Let's go back to the other place.'

'No. Have a beer here.'

'We'll go back afterwards then. No good being uncertain about it.'

When they got outside it was quite dark. They turned to the right of the door and started back towards the café where the man was.

'He's behind us,' Peter said. 'He must have been waiting outside.'

John looked round quickly. 'Yes, that looks like the same chap. What are we going to do?'

'We can't talk to anyone while he's with us. If he is following us it's to catch the French who are helping us. We'll have to drop him somehow.'

'Let's go to the place where we climbed out of the window.'

'We can't do it again. They'd be on us as soon as we walked in. I don't suppose they've repaired the lock yet anyway. Have to drop him somehow else. Let's separate.'

'O.K.,' John said. 'Where shall we meet?'

'Better not the Café d'Accordion in case we haven't manged to drop him. I'll see you outside the hotel at' – he looked at his watch – 'nine-thirty.'

'Right. We won't walk towards him. When we get to the next crossroads I'll go right and you go left. He may hesitate and then we stand a chance of losing him straight away. If we don't it's up to the one he follows.'

They walked on at the same pace until they reached the corner. Then they separated and began to walk fast. Peter turned to the left as soon as he could and then to the right and out on to the Bollwerk. There were a number of people about and he walked fast, threading his way between them and not looking back. Mustn't let him think I know I'm being followed. If he knows that they'll arrest us right away. He slowed down and began to fill his pipe. He filled it carefully and patted his pockets as though looking for matches. Pretending not to find any he turned and walked back the way he had come. As he turned he saw the figure of a man slip into a doorway.

He walked past the doorway without looking. He walked back to a café where he knew there was a permanent light burning on the counter for customers to light their cigarettes. He lit his pipe at the flame and came out of the café. He came out fast and turned in the direction he had been going in the first place, hoping to catch a glimpse of the man who was following him.

This time he did not see him and he walked on down

the Bollwerk. He crossed the bridge by the railway station and came out on to the road leading to Reiherwerder. There was a tram at the stop, just about to start. He ran the last hundred yards and caught the tram as it was gathering speed. The conductor caught his arm and shouted at him in German. He looked back but he could not see the man who was following.

He stood on the platform of the tram for two stops. At each stop there was a car close behind them and he thought it might be a car commandeered by his pursuer. At the third stop there was no car; so he got down off the tram and crossed the road. He caught the next tram going back into town. But he did not get off at the Bollwerk. He went right on into the town and made for the Hotel Sack where he stood waiting for John. I'd better not walk about, he thought. I'm safer standing still.

Punctually at nine-thirty he saw John coming down the street.

'He followed you,' John said. 'I stopped to light a cigarette and saw him chasing you down the road. Did you drop him all right?'

'Yes. I jumped a tram and gave him the slip. What do we do now?'

'Let's get out of this. The quicker we get out of here the better. Let's jump a train up to Danzig.'

'Seems a pity to waste all the contacts we've made. I thought we were getting somewhere at last. If we go up to Danzig we'll have to start all over again.'

'All right – we'll go up to the Café d'Accordion first,' John said. 'I don't fancy sleeping out tonight and we might be able to pick something up there. If we don't have any luck we'll go straight up to the goods yard and get right out of the place.'

The Café d'Accordion was full as ever. They ordered their drinks and stood by the bar, sizing up all the likely people there. Standing next to Peter was a man of his own age, a merchant seaman. He was drunk, rolling drunk, and he gabbled a mixture of German, French and English. He was trying to sell a boiler suit.

'How much?' John said in English. '*Wieviel?*'

The man turned round and stared at him solemnly.

'How much?' he said. 'I spik English, I spik German, I spik Dutch. I spik French, I spik all languages . . .' He stumbled forward and recovered himself. 'I tell you how much.' He pulled John forward and whispered drunkenly in his ear. 'I pinch 'em from a raumboot.' He flung an arm affectionately round John's shoulders. 'I pinch 'em from a raumboot tied alongside my dredger. Now I sell 'em, see? I spik English, I spik American, I spik . . .'

'What sort of boat are you from?' John spoke in English, but quietly.

The sailor did not want to talk quietly. 'I spik English, I spik German . . .'

Suddenly, he went out. Out like a light, flat on his face on the floor, down among the feet of the people at the bar. In falling he knocked a glass of beer from John's hand and it fell on top of him, soaking the back of his jacket and his hair.

Peter pulled John to one side.

'Don't get mixed up in it,' he said.

Someone had pulled the sailor to his feet and taken him away into a corner. Peter could still hear him shouting, 'I spik Swedish, I spik Russian, I spik German . . .'

'What is he?' he whispered.

'Swedish, I think,' John said.

'He's too drunk. Keep clear of him.'

'O.K.'

A waitress came by with a tray full of glasses of beer. As she passed, a young Frenchman put his arm round her waist and began to speak in burlesque German.

'*Ach, mein Liebe,*' he aid. '*Ach, mein Liebling, mein Liebschen.*'

She threw off his arm angrily.

'That's our man!' Peter said.

John looked at him. He was about twenty-five, tall and powerful-looking, with a dark face and brown angry eyes, a wide, full mouth, straight nose and tousled hair. He wore a scarf round his neck and his jacket was too short in the sleeves. He was sitting slouched back in his chair, a cigarette dangling from the corner of his mouth, just drunk enough to do and say as he pleased. He looked as though he usually did as he pleased. A man to help you if he thought he wanted to help you. Not a man to be frightened to help you.

'I'll wait until he goes to the lavatory,' he said.

When the Frenchman went out to the lavatory John followed. Presently they both came back into the room. John beckoned Peter over to the Frenchman's table and introduced him as René. He spoke no English, but Peter could tell by his voice he was going to help them. There was no doubt in that voice. It was a friendly, excited voice.

René called for a round of drinks and John told him the story of their stay in Stettin. He told him about the man who had been following them, because they did not want him to run any risks that he did not know about.

'You must come back to my camp,' René said. 'The air raid shelter is not safe. It is not safe to walk about the streets now. You must hide away until we can find you a ship. I know the barber – the English-speaking Frenchman, as you call him. He is a good man. He will find you a ship. In the meantime I and my friends will look. You must come with us. We will feed you and look after you until you can get away.

John turned to Peter and quickly translated what René had said. Thank God, Peter thought, thank God. At last, after all this time, we've found the man we're looking for.

He smiled at René and René smiled back and raised his thumb.

Then Peter glanced at the door, the quick, furtive glance round that he had laughed at in the Frenchmen but had unconsciously acquired himself. And in that quick glance he saw the man who had been following them.

He was standing with his back to the counter, watching them and drinking a glass of beer.

Peter felt a sudden anger, an anger against the fate that had lured them on with every promise of success only to let them down at the last minute. A thought flashed through his mind to murder the man, to kill him and throw his body into the sea. And then commonsense came to his rescue and a fatalism that had grown in him since he had been taken prisoner. They'd had a good run for it. The only thing was to submit now and go back quietly. There was no use in struggling against it. There was a time to struggle and a time to submit. They'd had a good try and now if they were lucky they would go back to the prison camp – to try again. It was always a matter of luck and the dice were so heavily loaded against the escaping prisoner. Once you were out of the camp it was all luck and they'd had it all with them for a time. And now it had turned against them. But he felt sick. He felt sick inside him with a desperate desire to go back in time. To turn back the clock and not make the mistakes that had brought the Gestapo on their track. He turned to John and tapped him on the knee.

'That chap who followed us is by the bar.'

John was talking to René and René was smiling. John said something quickly in French, but René did not stop smiling. He looked at the man by the counter and his smile grew broader.

The man's cool, Peter thought. He hasn't turned a hair. And he felt a sudden increase of faith in the man who sat there wearing the broad grin.

René got up and crossed over to the man at the bar. He said a few words and the man immediately left the café.

'What did you say to him?' John asked when René came back.

René laughed. 'That is the barber's brother. He has been following you to see that you do not get into trouble. Now we should return to the camp.'

Chapter Nine

They Meet Sigmund

They had some miles to walk before they got to René's camp, but they walked them cheerfully. This was no longer aimless walking. It was not walking because they dared not stay in one place, because they felt hunted and if they walked they felt less hunted. It was not walking round the docks, round the town, in search of Frenchmen whom they hardly expected to meet, and frightened all the time they would be stopped and their papers demanded. It was not walking because they were hungry and cold, and if they walked they felt less hungry and less cold. It was walking to get somewhere. It was walking openly and fast and they were cheerful because of that.

As they walked René explained why they had been followed. The man was a member of an anti-German organization – part of the organization to which the man who was going to Sweden belonged. Apparently André had not been completely satisfied with the result of the interrogation and so they had been followed; at first because André was suspicious, later for their own safety.

John asked him about the organization and he told them its real object was to preserve the morale of the French prisoners. It was not for action. They carried out a little negative sabotage; but the main purpose of the organization was to unite the prisoners in their hatred of the Boche and to keep alive the spirit of France.

'At the moment we can do nothing,' René said. 'We are powerless. But when the British invade, when the British drop us arms, then we shall rise.'

When they reached the camp they went in through the gate, this time openly. It was larger than the other, built as a labour camp and not as a prison. There was barbed wire, but as a gesture rather than as a defence. The huts were clean and dry; but they had the same smell, the same compounded smell of prison life. There were ten beds in René's room, ten lockers, and a table and some stools.

When Peter and John had been introduced they were given food, black German bread and lard-like margarine.

They did not talk much. They were tired. Soon after they had eaten the Frenchmen suggested that they should go to bed. They shared René's bed and he shared with another man. It was almost good to be back on the hard prison bed again; back in the live darkness of the crowded room, the friendly sound of sleeping men, and the sudden-glowing cigarettes.

They were awakened early in the morning, before it was light, when the Frenchmen dressed to go to work. They shared their breakfast of bread and margarine and ersatz coffee and were lighting their cigarettes when they heard footsteps outside. René tried to get them hidden under the beds, but before they could move the door burst open and a man stood panting inside the room.

It was the barber and when he could speak he spoke in French. He sat on the nearest stool and mopped his brow with a handkerchief.

John turned to Peter. 'He's fixed up for a boat to take us to Copenhagen.'

'Copenhagen? That's in Denmark.'

'Yes.'

'That's occupied by the Germans.'

'I know.'

'What's the use of that?'

'Well, it's somewhere.'

'We haven't any Danish papers. Or money.'

'We haven't any German left – so that's no argument. And we do stand a chance of getting help from the Danes. Besides, it'll be easier to get to Sweden from Denmark than from here.'

Peter thought it over. As usual John was all for going. All for going there and then; taking the risk and getting out of Germany. But Peter was cautious. He wanted to be certain they were not jeopardizing the ground they had already won. The longer they stayed out of the camp the more cautious he became, the more he wanted to hang on to what they had – even, sometimes, at the risk of not getting any farther.

He stood there undecided and the Frenchmen stood there in silence wondering at the delay.

'We can live here now,' Peter said. 'Why not stay here until we can get a boat to get us all the way?'

'We can't live on these chaps for ever!' John was growing impatient, not seeing the cause of Peter's doubt, not thinking about what they would do in Denmark, but thinking of getting there, of taking decisive action and getting out of the country.

'We can get in touch with the Resistance in Denmark,' he said.

'What do we do until then?' Peter asked. 'Sleep in the fields?'

'Well, I'm for going.' John was growing angry now, and obstinate.

'Ask them more about it. Ask them if the crew are staying in Denmark and if we can stay with them when we get there.'

John turned to the barber and spoke to him in French. The barber shrugged his shoulders as he replied.

'He doesn't know,' John said. 'He says the organization have arranged it. That's all he knows. He's come to take us to meet one of the crew.'

'We ought to make certain. It's taken us long enough to make this contact, and now as soon as we've made it you want to go dashing off to Denmark. Getting caught in Denmark is no better than getting caught in Germany. It's no use dashing off after the first red herring that comes along.'

'How do you know it's a red herring? I should think it's pretty easy to get across from Denmark into Sweden. We might find it easier to steal a small boat there. Anyway, it's better than going up to Danzig.'

'O.K. Let's meet him and see what he has to say.'

John turned again to the Frenchman and then to Peter.

'We're to meet him in an hour's time outside the Café d'Accordion.'

An hour later they were awaiting the arrival of the Danish sailor. They did not wait outside the door of the café, but farther down the road where they could watch the meeting-place.

They waited for ten minutes after the agreed time, but the sailor did not come. They began to feel alarmed and were about to return to the camp when they were accosted by a young man wearing a neat blue overcoat. He looked like a student.

'Good morning.' He said it in passable English.

'Good morning,' Peter said.

'I have come to take you aboard my ship. I have one spare pass. I can take one of you and return for the other.'

215

'What happens when we get to Denmark?' Peter asked, feeling ungrateful as he said it.

'When you get to Denmark you will be all right.'

'Where shall we stay? How soon can we get to Sweden?'

'When you get to Denmark you can easily reach Sweden from there. People go from Denmark to Sweden all the time. From Germany it is not so easy.'

'He's right, Pete.' John wanted to stir him. Wanted him to see the advantage of this as he himself saw it, clearly and without alternative.

'Where will you hide us in the ship?' Peter asked and John stood by feeling embarrassed. He felt embarrassed as he had felt when he had gone shopping in Exeter with his aunt and she, after years in India, had haggled with the shopkeeper. Had tried to beat down the price that was as fixed and unassailable as the ancient town itself.

'They'll hide us all right,' he said. 'They'll know where to put us.'

'We sail this afternoon,' the Dane said.

'We'd better go, Pete.'

'Who's going first?' Peter asked, accepting it grudgingly. 'You can if you like.'

'No fear!' John said. 'You go first.' He turned to the Dane. 'I'll wait here for you.' To Peter, 'You'll only get into conversation with someone if I leave you here alone.'

They had no difficulty in getting into the docks. The Dane made Peter walk in front of him, along through the gate into the dock, and then caught up with him and said, 'Follow me, but do not come too close. Follow me up the gangplank and do not look at anyone. Do not come too close. If I stop to talk to anyone walk past us and slow down until I come.'

Peter followed him down the quayside, openly and in daylight where they had gone before furtively and in the dark. They came to the quay where the Danish ship was berthed. She was called the *S.I. Norensen*. There was a gangplank down and on the other side of the quay Russian soldiers were loading a ship under the supervision of a German guard.

The Dane walked up the gangplank, crossed the deck and vanished down a companionway. Peter followed and found himself in the forecastle. The Dane motioned him to a seat without speaking and went out again by the companionway.

Peter sat in the dark cabin waiting for the Dane to return with John. He looked round him at the triangular cabin, lined with two-tier bunks. The apex of the triangle was the bows of the ship. At the base of the triangle was a cast-iron stove and a long table ran down the centre between the bunks.

He wanted the ship to be at sea. To feel the roll and lurch of it and to know that it was taking them away from Germany. He crossed to one of the portholes and looked out on to the docks. The German sentry had his back to the ship and was watching the Russians. John and the Dane were walking unconcernedly along the quay. It's going to be O.K., he thought, we're going to make it.

Then John and the Dane were in the forecastle and the three of them stood round the cast-iron stove warming their hands.

'You will be home soon,' the Dane said. 'You will be home for Christmas maybe.'

Peter looked at John. Home for Christmas. What had been a dream was becoming real. What had seemed a fantastic shot against long odds was now a possibility. And the nearer they came to winning through the more nervous he became. They were now in someone else's hands. They had no decisions to make until they were ashore again. Just do as they were told and ride it out. Ride it out patiently while the others did the thinking. And were the others competent? Their necks were at

217

stake. All their necks were at stake now except his and John's, but he did not like trusting them. While he and John went their own way, while they stayed alone and worked together, he did not mind. If they lost it they lost it themselves and had no one to blame for it. At first it had been John who had wanted to go alone, John who had not wanted the contact with the French, who had not wanted to accept the risk involved in speaking to them in the streets; he had wanted to go on alone, to stow away or steal a boat, but to travel alone and not depend on the French.

But now it was both of them. They had done what they could. They had gone as far as they could go alone. They had depended on the French and now they were depending on the Danes. They could do nothing about it now. They could just ride it out and leave the decisions to others. And he was nervous because of this.

Then Larensen came in. Larensen was the crew boss and had been ashore. He was a big man. Big, dark and fleshy with a stubble of black beard and a face that showed red and fleshy through the stubble. His eyes were blue and bloodshot and he smelled of schnapps. He was drunk, affectionately drunk.

'You boys will be all right now. I'm Larensen, see?' He spoke English with an American accent. 'Call me Olaf. I see you all right. I'm de head man around here. I send Sigmund for you, see? I fix everything. You don't have to worry now.'

He turned to John. 'You an aviator?'

'No,' said John. 'I'm in the army.'

'In the army, eh?' He pulled a bottle of schnapps from his coat pocket. 'You boys like a drink, eh?' He took out the cork and wiped the top of the bottle with his hand before offering it to John. 'What do you do before the war?'

John took a drink from the bottle before replying. 'I was at university.'

'A professor, eh?' He turned to Peter. 'He's too young to be a professor.'

'He was a student,' Peter explained.

'He was a professor,' Larensen said.

'All right,' Peter said, 'he was a professor.'

The rest of the crew came in one by one and then they were all there. They did not seem surprised that there were strangers in the forecastle. They came in one by one until there were five of them. Five young men, almost boys, dressed in cheap smart suits and overcoats. As they came in they each took a drink from the bottle of schnapps. They changed from their smart clothes into sweaters and overalls and became at once men and more dependable. Sigmund, the man who had brought them aboard, altered most with the change of clothes. He wore a heavy knitted Scandinavian sea jersey and assumed authority with it.

When the crew had changed they sat round the table in the forecastle drinking schnapps while the cabin boy fried eggs and bacon on the cast-iron stove. Peter sat there with his back against one of the bunks drinking schnapps from the bottle and smelling the bacon as it was cooking. One of the crew gave him a cigarette, but he could not smoke. His stomach was turning over and he was nearly sick from the smell of the frying bacon and the sound of sizzling and spluttering in the pan.

It's quite true, he thought, your mouth does water. He sat there trying to talk to Larensen until the boy placed a plate of eggs and bacon on the table in front of him. He passed it to John and Larensen cut them thick slices of white bread from the loaf on the table. Then his plate came up and Larensen sat watching them as they ate, eating quickly and thoroughly and wiping their plates with bread when they had finished.

'You boys were hungry, eh?' Larensen went to a

cupboard at the end of the forecastle and came back with a large piece of cake on a plate. 'Made from eggs,' he said. 'Our last cargo was of eggs. Eggs for Germany.' He made a short explosive sound with his lips.

They slept on the bunks while the crew made the ship ready for sea. About two o'clock Larensen woke them with tea and sandwiches and told them that the Germans were coming to search the ship before she sailed. He sat opposite them at the small forecastle table while they ate the food. His two mahogany-coloured, dirt-grained and calloused hands rested on the edge of the table. One of the fingers of his right hand was missing.

'You boys eat good!' he told them. 'Presently you go down in the bilge. We put in for an inspection first thing in the morning. We have another search at Swinemünde and that's the last of Germany. After that we go straight to Copenhagen.'

'Are there many Germans in Copenhagen?' Peter asked.

'Sure, hundreds. You ask Sigmund all about the Germans. He'll tell you. He's a fire-eater. He wants to eat all the Germans there are. He wants to throw 'em all into the sea. He's a dangerous guy.'

'Is he one of the crew?'

'He's a contact man for the underground organization. He sails with us as a deckhand. He sails with us too long now. Soon he will be caught. He takes might' big risks, that feller.'

Larensen slid aside a panel in the apex of the triangle that was the forecastle. Behind the panel was a small cubby-hole formed in the extreme bows of the ship. It was just large enough to hold the two of them and smelled of paint and sea-water. The walls were the steel walls of the ship, and they were cold and water condensed and dripped from them.

They squeezed into the cubby-hole and Larensen passed

them a wooden box to sit on, a torch, a bottle of water, an empty bottle and a metal funnel.

'You may be there some hours,' he said. 'Don't shine the torch if you hear voices and don' speak unless I open the door. The Germans will come down here but they won' use tear gas in the fo'c'sle. I give 'em a drink, see? I give 'em a drink in the fo'c'sle, so you keep very quiet. If you make a noise' – he drew his hand across his throat in a cutting gesture – 'and don' smoke, or you cough. I fix 'em, see? I fix 'em good. If the dog comes down here I fix 'im too. I got pepper to fix 'im. I fix 'im good.'

He replaced the panel, leaving them in the darkness of the cubby-hole. John shone the torch and they settled themselves to wait. It was cold and in spite of their mackintoshes and heavy woollen underwear they shivered.

They stayed there for several hours, unable to talk and apprehensive of every step on the deck above. Once they heard the sound of military boots and the whining of a dog and then German voices shouting on the quay. Then there was silence. They began to feel stiff and were tempted to tap on the panel in front of them. They had filled the empty bottle and the cold was becoming unbearable. Waves of coldness came from the wet steel hull, numbing their limbs and deadening their minds.

Escape is all coldness, Peter thought. Coldness and waiting. It's heat sometimes in digging and in running away. But mostly it's coldness and hunger and hanging about waiting.

They heard the Germans come below into the cabin. They heard the unnecessarily loud voice of Larensen talking German and the laughter and the sound of a glass against a bottle. And the heavy dragging movement as the soldiers eased themselves into the seat that ran along underneath the bunks.

Peter sat there riding it out. He had forgotten the

221

cold now and the fact that his bladder was full. He was listening for the sound of the German voices and for the sniffing of the dogs. He thought he heard it once but he could not be certain. They had put out the torch and through the darkness he could feel John's tenseness as he crouched down beside him, listening to the voices in the cabin on the other side of the wooden partition.

Then he heard them leaving, heard the triumphant note in Larensen's voice as he saw them out of the forecastle, heard their feet trampling across the deck and heard Larensen come back into the cabin and squeeze past the seat to remove the panel.

'I gottem,' he said. 'I fixed 'em. We have something to eat now, then I hide you down below. The German guard, look, look, here! See?' He took them over to a porthole. There was a German soldier standing at the bottom of the gangplank. 'When we sail he come with us as far as Swinemünde. We drop 'im off at Swinemünde and then you can come up here. But now you have something to eat and then go down below, eh?'

He got them more sandwiches of dry bread and bacon and led them down through a trap door in the floor of the forecastle on to the deck below, down through another trap door, forward and down through another trap door; and forward again into the bilges where the anchor chain was stored.

'Be careful of the chain,' he said. 'Keep away from that chain when the anchor goes down. It goes down at Swinemünde. When the anchor goes down you know you won't have to wait long.' He left them a storm lantern and the fat bacon sandwiches and went back up the ladder. They could hear the trap doors banging as he climbed into the forecastle.

They found a canvas sea-anchor in a corner and made themselves a bed. It was cold in the bilge, colder than it had been in the cubby-hole, but they could move and

222

stamp their feet and beat their arms across their backs to keep them warm. Peter ate his share of the sandwiches and fell asleep.

Some time later he was wakened by the slowing-down of the engines and they knew that they had reached Swinemünde. They crouched in a corner as far away as they could from the anchor chain. Then the engines died and the anchor went down, the chain plunging and kicking like a wild animal as it crashed around in the small compass of the locker. It stopped and they heard the gentle lap, lap of the waves against the hull. It was deathly silent in the locker after the thump of the engines and the clatter and the bang of the running anchor chain.

This is the last check, Peter thought. If we pass this one we get to Denmark.

They lay on the hard canvas of the sea-anchor listening to the lapping of the water and imagining the pilot and the guard leaving the ship, and the captain taking over. They could hear nothing but the lapping of the water on the hull and an occasional thump that they thought might be the pilot boat pushing off.

Then the anchor came up and the engines started again. And they began to move and they knew that they would get to Denmark.

Chapter Ten

The Danish Resistance

Peter woke suddenly and completely. It was quite dark. He reached for the torch in the side pocket of his mackintosh and flashed it on his wrist. His watch had stopped.

He sent the thin beam of light cutting across the darkness of the locker. John lay sleeping with his head on his arm, his long lashes dark over his cheeks and a slight smile on his unshaven face.

They had been sick during the night. Peter shifted his weight uncomfortably on the hard canvas. His mouth tasted foul and his lips were dry and cracked. They had been sick until they had fallen asleep from sheer exhaustion. The lamp had burned itself out and it had been dark. Peter had been sick before, he had been sick on the sea and in the air. But he had never been as sick as this. The sea had been rough and the water in the bilge had swished and rolled, filling the locker with the smell of all the refuse of the years.

It had not been so bad while they had the storm lantern. But when the oil ran out and they were left in the darkness, unable to see one another but hearing the groans and falling cascades of one another's sickness, then the locker had become a black, damp, tossing, stinking hell.

He heard footsteps on the deck above and Larensen came down the ladder bringing with him a jug of coffee and some sandwiches. He was sober now and told them that there was no longer any danger of their being boarded.

'I had to leave you boys in the locker,' he said, 'because of the coast patrol. You been sick, professor?'

John looked at Peter. 'He wants to know if we've been sick.'

An hour later Sigmund came down with a lantern and took them up to the forecastle. 'You will be more comfortable here,' he said. 'You can sleep in the bunks for the next two nights and then you will have to go down in the bilges again. It is not very comfortable down there, I think.'

224

'It's not too bad,' John said. 'We're not used to the movement yet.'

'It will get worse,' Sigmund said. 'We get very rough crossings at this time of the year. It will be better when we are among the islands.'

'Where shall we go when we get to Copenhagen?' Peter asked.

'You will either be hidden in the town or you will come with me to the Resistance. It will depend on the sailors. Sometimes our boats have to hide because of German patrols. We must wait until we reach Copenhagen before we know. It will be arranged. You are with us now. It is for Mr Olsen to decide.'

'Who's Mr Olsen?'

'There is no such person as Mr Olsen. It is the name we give to the leader of the Resistance. I do not know his real name. I do not wish to talk about the Resistance.'

They spent the rest of the day sitting in the forecastle playing cards, sleeping and eating the eggs and bacon that Larensen cooked on the small cast-iron stove. As Sigmund had predicted, the weather worsened as the day passed and by the evening the ship was rolling so much that the two passengers were glad to climb into their bunks.

The next day was just as rough. They could not eat breakfast but lay in their bunks waiting for the time to pass. Now they had time to think about the future. To Peter, sick as he was, it seemed that in Denmark they would be little better off than they had been in Germany. In Denmark they would be in the hands of the Resistance Movement. They would act without knowing the cause or the meaning of their actions. They would merely do as they were told, without knowing or considering the wisdom of what they did. He decided to cut their stay in Denmark as short as possible.

During the next two days Sigmund told them of the

German occupation of Denmark. How at first the Germans had been 'correct', hoping to make a peaceful conquest of the country, taking their food for the German army and using only a small part of that army as a force of occupation. But the Danish people had refused to cooperate. There had been clashes in the streets at night. Some German soldiers had been killed. Hostages had been taken and a curfew declared. Now, no Danes were allowed out of their houses after eight o'clock at night and many of the younger people had withdrawn to the country where they waged guerrilla warfare against the Germans.

'We are mostly students,' Sigmund told them. 'Only those who can no longer work in the open live in the country. The life of a contact man is not long. After a few trips he becomes known to the Jerries. Then it is a matter of luck whether he is recalled before he is sent to a concentration camp or shot. I have had luck. This is my last journey. When I reach Copenhagen I shall go to the country.'

On the morning of the third day Sigmund, who had been up on the bridge, came down to the forecastle.

'We have had a code radio from Mr Olsen!' he said. 'The Jerries are waiting to arrest me when we get to Copenhagen. Mr Olsen is sending a small boat out to pick me up before we get in. We shall alter the ship's log so that my name is not there. You will come with me.'

'Where shall we go?' Peter asked.

'To the country. It seems there has been much trouble in Copenhagen. Many have been arrested. There will be much to do.'

'How will they take us off in a small boat?' Peter asked.

'It will be difficult. The captain has been given a rendezvous. The ship docks early tomorrow morning.

During the night we shall meet the boat and she will take us off. If we miss her, we are all finished. For myself, I shall go overboard during the night and try to swim to the shore. It will be better than a concentration camp.'

'We could take a lifeboat,' John suggested.

'That we cannot do. They would see that a boat was missing and shoot the captain. We shall not appear on the books and it will not involve him. But we cannot take a boat.'

They spent the rest of the day and the night waiting anxiously for the boat. The wind was rising and they were both sick again.

Before daybreak the engines slowed down and they went on deck. There was a heavy sea running and it was raining. The wind breaking the tops of the waves sent a fine spray of salt water sweeping across the ship. The rain was slanting down as a solid sheet; but the sea spray was horizontal, a fine stinging horizontal spray of drenching wetness. The sky was a few feet above the sea, solid and black, and the wind howled through the rigging as the ship nosed down into the sea.

'It's a bit rough!' Peter shouted. 'Never get a small boat out in this.'

They stood by the rail, the spray stinging in their faces, straining their eyes for a sight of the boat.

'I don't like it,' John said. 'We'll never swim in this.'

The ship was rolling in the sea like an old tub. In the faint light of the early morning they could see the white-crested waves riding past them, breaking and blowing and spraying in the wind. At one moment the ship was poised forty feet in the air and in the next she was sinking down, down, as though she would never rise again. But she did rise, shaking the sea from her decks and wallowing on, her engines barely giving her steering way.

'There she is!' Sigmund shouted.

Peter had just time to see a red star shell curve down into the sea. 'They'll have the coastal patrol on us!' he said.

As he spoke there was a swoosh behind him and a rocket went rushing up into the night. There was an answering star shell from the boat and then they could see her tossing like a cork on the waves.

'We will have to jump,' Sigmund said. 'They will not get alongside in a sea like this.' He went down to the forecastle and returned with three lifebelts. 'Wear these. We will jump one by one. Do not jump until you see they have picked up the man before you. You go first!' he told John.

The boat came round to their lee side. She carried a small searchlight which she played on the water between them.

'Over you go!' Sigmund ordered.

John held his nose and jumped. He fell into the water between the ship's side and the boat and was hauled on board as the boat fell rapidly astern. Presently she was up with them again.

'You next!' Sigmund said.

Peter climbed the rail and stood looking down on the black sea. Choosing the moment when the ship was in a trough he jumped far out from the side of the ship towards the boat.

The sea was not cold at first. But then the coldness gripped him. He struck out for the boat, wildly, his lungs full of salt water, terrified and clumsy. They had some difficulty pulling him into the boat. Then he was lying in the bottom of the boat and someone was forcing brandy between his teeth.

Sigmund joined them in the bottom of the boat. The engine was put to 'full ahead' and they were plunging and bouncing towards the shore.

228

They came to the land at first light. The wind had abated slightly but there was a fast sea running and the sky was low and angry. It was a bleak and desolate coastline, great black cliffs rising from the grey sea with a surf line that showed white and angry at their base.

The two men who were the boat's crew sat silent as she plunged and quivered to the pounding sea. The three passengers lay wet and shivering under a pile of blankets in the well.

As they came to the shore, Sigmund spoke in Danish to the man who was steering.

The man replied, also in Danish. He was a quiet man, bleached and tanned by the sea.

'They have caught Mr Olsen,' Sigmund said. 'The Jerries have caught Mr Olsen.' He said it as though it meant the end of the Resistance.

'How?' Peter asked. He did not care much about Mr Olsen at the moment. He was cold and sick and he wanted to get to the shore.

'The Jerries raided the farm where he was staying. They have put him in prison.'

They came round in a wide sweep in the bay and ran into a narrow fjord where there was a strip of white beach and a steep path to the top of the cliff. They could smell the seaweed as they came in, strong and heady in the early morning freshness, and the gulls soared and swooped above them, screaming and turning their heads to watch the boat as she ran in to the rough jetty at the bottom of the cliff.

The steersman spoke again to Sigmund.

'We must go quickly,' Sigmund translated. 'There are bicycles at the top of the cliff. These men will hide the boat. There are German patrols. We must not waste time.'

They climbed the steep path to the top of the cliff, their clothes hanging damply to them as they climbed. By the time they reached the top they were warm, and steam rose from them as they stood looking at the orderly countryside.

It was a toy landscape. A landscape of neat houses, trim fields and well-kept roads. There were no hedges, but wooden fences and earthen walls.

Three bicycles stood at the top of the path, chained together and fastened by a padlock which Sigmund unlocked with the key given to him by the boatman. 'We will ride fast. It is getting late.'

He led them inland down the smooth tarmac roads, riding oddly on the right-hand side of the road. They were strange heavy bicycles, with thick tyres and upturned handlebars, but it was better than walking and the rush of the wind was drying their clothes. Then the sun came out, weakly at first but growing warmer, and the blood moved in them and for the first time since leaving Germany they felt free.

Sigmund led them at a fast pace. He led them for several hours, past hamlets and villages without stopping; shouting greetings to the villagers, but pressing on all the time, urgent, anxious to get to the Resistance and hear the news of Mr Olsen.

Peter was not urgent. The sun was shining and he was reluctant to involve himself in the troubles of the Resistance Movement. He wanted to get away. The Resistance was a side issue, an incident in the main scheme of the escape, and he wanted to make that incident as short as possible. His clothes were dry now and he was enjoying the ride across the strange and lovely countryside.

The storm had passed, leaving a sky of clear blue against which the faint streaks of high cirrus floated like silver smoke. The roads were straight and lined with trees, and in the villages the houses were painted pink and white and pale blue, and huge beech trees with their bare branches guarded the quiet streets.

They stopped outside one of the villages, at a small farm which lay back off the road.

'This is the headquarters,' Sigmund told them. 'Wait here till I report.'

He handed his bicycle to John and knocked at the door. DIT DIT DIT DAH, the V sign.

A woman came to the door. She was an old woman, dressed in peasant costume. Her face was brown and red and her hair was tied in a coloured handkerchief.

Sigmund came back to the road again. 'They have gone. We must ride some more miles.'

They mounted their bicycles again and rode on. Peter was not interested in the countryside any more. He was stiff and saddle-sore and he wanted to get to wherever they were going as soon as possible. He was hungry and thirsty and his clothes were irritating where the salt had dried in them.

The new headquarters was in a large farmhouse. Of brick this time, with a thatched roof and huge old-fashioned chimneys.

There was a sentry standing at the gates, a young man wearing British battledress trousers, a sweater and sea-boots. On his head he wore a black cap with a shiny peak to it and he was armed with a Thompson sub-machine-gun and a revolver in a leather holster which he wore tied cowboy-fashion to his leg.

Sigmund spoke to him in Danish. The sentry saluted and stepped to one side as they went in through the gate.

They entered the farmhouse and found themselves in a low room with a stone floor and a heavy beamed ceiling. There was a large tiled stove at one end of the room and in the centre a long trestle table at which three men were sitting. The room was like an armoury. Service rifles stood in wooden racks against the far wall and beneath them were boxes of ammunition and open trays full of hand grenades. To the left of the rifles stood a small table on which was a grey British transmitting and receiving set. On the table where the men were sitting lay four Browning machine-guns.

The men looked up as the three of them came into the room. They were all armed.

Sigmund spoke to them in Danish. He spoke fast. Peter heard the letters R.A.F. repeated several times.

The men stood up. Their faces had brightened as Sigmund spoke.

'R.A.F.,' the man at the head of the table said in unaccustomed English. 'You are welcome to our country. It is good to see the R.A.F.'

'This is Carl,' Sigmund said. 'He is Mr Olsen's second-in-command.'

Carl was a tall man in his late forties. Grey and thin but with keen eyes and steady hands.

'You are welcome,' he said again.

'Thank you,' Peter said. He looked at the other two men. They were both young. They looked like students. He walked over to the table. 'Browning guns!' He took up one of the guns, holding its well-known shape, brown and slightly oily, in his hands.

'It will not fire,' Carl said.

Peter turned the gun over. 'Number one stoppage,' he said. 'We ought to be able to fix that.'

The men watched Peter as he stripped the gun. It was good to see the stripped gun coming to pieces in his hands, to see the clean and oiled parts placed in neat rows on the wooden table. He stripped the gun down to the breech block.

'Bad luck. Broken firing pin.'

'You can fix it?' Carl asked.

'Not unless you have a spare breech block,' Peter told him.

Carl crossed to a pile of sacking in the corner of the

room and returned with a Browning gun, its barrel bent and twisted by fire.

'Where did you get them?' John asked.

'From a crashed R.A.F. bomber,' Carl said. 'We got there before the Germans did. All the crew were dead. We gave them a military funeral. They are buried in the local churchyard. We got the guns and the ammunition away.'

Peter was stripping the damaged gun. 'Good show!' he said. 'The breech is O.K. We can fix the gun for you all right.'

'That is good,' Carl said. 'We have made stands for them. We shall use them against the Germans.'

They had eaten their meal, all sitting together at the long table and eating the roast goose and vegetables from the farm, with weak Danish beer and good white bread made by the farmer's wife. Carl had taken Sigmund to another room, leaving the four young men sitting at the table. The Danes spoke good English and the talk had been of their weapons. They carried an assortment of Danish, German and Finnish arms, but these were the first Browning guns they had seen and they were keen to know how they were fixed.

'There are right- and left-hand feeds,' Peter explained. 'They're made that way to fit into the gun turrets. To change them over you do this.' He showed them how to adapt the feed of the guns.

'How do you load them?' one of the Danes asked. He was a tall, fair-haired youth with spectacles, and they called him Hans.

'First you make up the belt' – Peter showed them how to fit the cartridges together to form the belt – 'always keeping the smooth side of the clip to the same side of the belt. The belt you found in the aircraft will be composed of assorted rounds in the following order:

armour-piercing, incendiary, explosive, solid and tracer.'
Saying this, he was carried back to a small wooden
hut on an airfield in England. There was the sound
of revving engines outside the hut, and inside a class of
bored navigators were half-listening to the instructor who,
parrot-fashion, ran through the patter from the armament
manual.

'You'll use the bullets you need for the particular
job you're doing,' he continued. 'The tracer won't be
much good, but the incendiaries should be very useful
for sabotage work.' He showed them how to tell the type
of bullet by the colour of the roundels on the base of the
cartridges.

'What of the cooling of them?' the second student
asked. He was a short young man with a mop of dark
curly hair. He looked Jewish.

'You'll have to fire it in short bursts. They're air-cooled
and were designed to fire in the air. They'll be all right
if you fire short bursts as you would with a Tommy-gun.
Otherwise they'll jam.'

'We shall use them in the raid on the jail,' Hans
said. 'If we had known how to work them earlier they
would not have caught Mr Olsen. We shall rescue him
tonight.'

'How was he caught?' John asked.

'After a raid,' the Jewish one told him. 'It was a
good raid, a raid on a transformer in Copenhagen. We
got away by lorry and threw spikes on the road as we
flew. It was a good raid and we all got away.'

'It was after this raid that they caught Mr Olsen,'
Hans said. 'He was seen by one of the Schalburg Corps
who recognized him and informed the Jerries.'

'The Schalburg Corps?' John asked.

'A section of the Danish Nazi Party. They were organized to counteract the activities of the Resistance Movement. Being Danes, they are more dangerous to us than

234

the German military. They are traitors and between us there is war to the death. The fight between us and the Schalburg Corps is worse than that between us and the Germans. It is hard now to think of one's life before the Germans came. I have been fighting now for more than a year. My mother and sister are in Copenhagen but I have not been to my home for a year. I cannot see my mother or the Germans would take her. My brother has been sent to a concentration camp in Germany.'

'My father was shot,' the Jew said. 'They shot him because he was a Jew. My mother got away and is in Sweden.'

'We got five hundred Jews to Sweden last month,' Hans said.

'How do you take them?' Peter asked. This was what he wanted. What he had been waiting for.

'In small boats. We take them over the Straits at night.'

'What about the German patrols?'

'We dodge them. We know the waters and use the wind. I enjoyed doing that. We were entertained well in Sweden.'

'Can you get us across like that?'

'We will see Carl,' Hans said. 'He is in charge while Mr Olsen is not here. But first we have to rescue Mr Olsen.'

That afternoon Sigmund took them by train to Copenhagen. 'I am taking you to my sister,' he said. 'You must do exactly as she says and make no noise. If I should not return for you, you must wait there until one of us makes contact with you. On no account must you leave the flat.'

He walked them by a roundabout route through a maze of similar streets and stopped outside a block of flats. He rang one of the bells and went in through the swing doors and up the concrete stairs. Peter and John followed him to one of the flats on the third floor landing.

The door was opened by a tall, fair girl. She looked frightened. Sigmund spoke to her in Danish and she closed her eyes. Her face went white but she smiled and motioned them into the room.

Chapter Eleven

The Last Enemy

It was a small room with modern furniture, plain cream walls and green plants in boxes under the window and trailing from small shelves fixed to the wall. It was quiet and there was an air of feminine order about it. Peter felt strange and uncouth in this room – the first private room he had entered for a year. He felt that he was bringing dirt and danger into this girl's flat, and he did not like it.

Sigmund had not introduced them. He had spoken in Danish to the girl, warned them again not to leave the flat and had gone; leaving them standing awkwardly, facing the frightened girl across the table.

The girl's fear was obvious. She was tall and fair, and now her face was pale. Her large eyes betrayed her fear. It was a fear that was new to Peter and it disturbed him.

John spoke first. 'It's good of you to have us here.' A stock opening gambit which sounded lame as he said it.

The girl said something in Danish.

'She doesn't speak English,' Peter said.

John tried again in French, but the girl still replied in Danish and shook her head. He tried German, but she still could not understand. So they stood there awkwardly. Standing because the girl was standing and hoping that she would sit.

Peter took a chair and placed it behind her. She smiled and they sat on opposite sides of the table.

The girl seemed helpless with fear. Peter wondered whether she was frightened of them or of the danger they had brought with them. This was difficult. What could they do? There was a wireless set standing in the corner of the room. He pointed to it and said 'England?'

The girl nodded. She took a portable gramophone from a shelf and put on a dance record. Then she crossed to the radio and tuned in, very faintly, to England. It seemed a well-worn routine. In Germany, among the French, it would have been furtive. Here, encircled by the girl's fear, it seemed a reasonable precaution.

Peter and John crouched down, ear to the loudspeaker, while the girl played dance music on the gramophone. It was the B.B.C. – the calm, unemotional voice of an announcer reading the news. England seemed very near to them then. Very near and very real.

When the news was finished the girl put on her hat and coat. She traced her finger round the dial of her watch to tell them that she would be gone for an hour.

While she was away they washed themselves and shaved. Then they fell asleep in their chairs, sitting one each side of the electric fire.

In the evening she woke them with cups of apple-leaf tea.

'Even if she doesn't speak English she knows the good old teatime,' John said.

She had brought a Danish-English dictionary with her. She told them to take off their shoes so that their footsteps could not be heard in the flat below. She played the radio to drown their conversation. She played the radio all the time, so that they began to feel nervous if it was not playing.

The girl was frightened all the time. Every time a door opened, or she heard footsteps on the pavement below, she started nervously in her chair and only relaxed when the footsteps had died away in the distance.

This fear was new to Peter. In the camp the prisoners had not been afraid of the Germans. You might be shot escaping, but that was a risk of war. In escaping he had not been frightened like this. That had been the hot, exhilarating fear of excitement. This was the cold, pervasive fear of the Gestapo, the fear of informers, the helpless fear of the civilian under military rule. This girl's fear was of torture, of whips and the horror of the concentration camp. The fear of being taken away to an unknown but imagined fate.

It was infectious. For the first time since leaving the camp Peter began to regret its security, began to admit their danger in being outside the camp. He wanted to get away from this girl, away from the fear in which she lived.

He helped her wash the teacups in the small kitchen and went back into the lounge where John was trying to get the B.B.C. on the radio.

'That kid's scared,' Peter said.

'So am I,' John told him. 'I'd much rather be outside then cooped up like this.'

'I don't like being involved with these people,' Peter said. 'If we're caught on our own we're caught and it's all clear-cut. And we know what's coming to us. But if we get caught with a crowd like this there's no knowing where we'll end up.'

'It's a risk we've got to take. I don't like it any more than you, but we've got to trust them, I suppose.'

'It's not that I don't trust them. I don't like not knowing what's going on. It's depending on someone we don't know that frightens me. What happens if the raid goes wrong and they're all arrested or killed?'

'They'll be all right,' John said. 'Sigmund will come back for us. Be in Sweden before we know where we are.'

'Hope to God you're right – I hope he comes soon. Can't stand much more of this hanging around.'

They slept that night in the flat and the following morning Sigmund returned. One of his hands was bandaged.

'How did it go?' John asked.

'It was O.K.,' Sigmund said. 'We got Mr Olsen all right. We killed several Jerries.'

'What have you done to your hand?'

'It is a bullet wound. It was a good raid. Now we go. We shall try to get you away tonight. We must go now to meet Larensen.'

'How shall we go?' Peter asked.

'We shall go in the same ship. She docked last night. Now I am to take you on board again. She will pass down the Swedish coast on her way back to Germany and arrangements will be made to put you ashore.'

'How will they do it?' Peter asked.

'It will be arranged,' Sigmund assured him. 'When they enter neutral waters they take a Swedish pilot aboard and drop him again when they leave neutral waters. Arrangements will be made for you to go ashore with the pilot.'

'How shall we get into the docks?' Peter asked.

'That also has been arranged. You will use the passes of two of the crew. The same was done for a prisoner called Rowe. He was taken from Danzig in a Swedish ship.'

Peter turned to John. 'Phil! He beat us to it.'

'That was the one you were telling me about,' Sigmund said, 'the one who escaped with you?'

'He followed us out,' Peter said. 'We never thought he'd make it.'

'I bet he thinks we're back at Sagan,' John said. 'I bet he's written to us already.'

'We'll see him soon.' Peter grinned. 'That'll shake 'im.'

'We have to go now,' Sigmund told him.

They all stood up.

'Thank your sister for us,' Peter said. 'Tell her we think she is very brave.'

Sigmund spoke with his sister.

'She thanks you,' he interpreted, 'and wishes me to tell you that she is not brave. She is glad to help those who are fighting to liberate our country. But she is frightened all the time.'

'Tell her she's not the only one,' Peter said. 'Tell her we're scared too.'

Sigmund translated, and the girl smiled her disbelief. She held out her hand and they left her watching them from the top of the narrow stairs.

Whenever Peter saw Sigmund in his shore-going clothes he lost faith in him. Sigmund on board ship and Sigmund ashore were two different people. Afloat, in his narrow trousers and thick natural-wool jersey, he was strong. A man of rough sympathy to be depended on because he was not seasick. But ashore, in his white collar and cheap blue tie, walking uncomfortably in tight shoes, he was frightening. Peter had no faith in Sigmund ashore. He had no faith in Larensen either.

They had their lunch in a large café in the centre of Copenhagen. It was crowded. They were handed menu cards as large as foolscap and ate oysters, chicken and ice cream. While they ate, a dance band played English dance tunes and the crooner sang the words in English.

But all the time they were nervous. There were German soldiers sitting round them and they could not talk. They had meant it to be a celebration for Philip, but it was not a celebration. It was too soon to celebrate.

Then they went to meet Larensen. Sigmund took them down into the dock area past the wooden fishing vessels and down among the high walls of the warehouses. As they were walking they heard a muffled explosion to the north of the town.

'Do you hear?' Sigmund said.

'Yes. What was it?'

'Sabotage.'

'How do you know?'

'That was the power station. We had arranged to blow it up today.'

Peter and John walked on in silence. If it were so it was tremendous. They found it hard to believe.

Then they saw Larensen. Even from that distance they could see he was drunk. He was reeling along the pavement and there was a woman with him, supporting him.

As soon as he saw them he began to shout. 'Hey, professor! Hey, Peter!'

He came towards them shouting in English and waving his arms.

Peter said, 'Sigmund, can't you keep him quiet?'

'I will go to talk with him,' Sigmund said.

They slowed down and watched him as he hurried forward. They saw him stop in front of Larensen and reason with him. Sigmund, his coat open and a new brown felt hat respectably on his head, reasoned with Larensen, fleshy and confident, dressed in dirty sea-going clothes, a scarf knotted round his throat and his woman clinging to his arm. They saw Larensen fling his free arm round Sigmund's shoulders and the three of them walk up the road staggering with the weaving of Larensen's progress and trying to keep him quiet.

'Hey, Peter,' he called. 'Professor, come here!' And

he laughed and hugged Sigmund round the shoulders.

'Let's get out of this,' John urged.

'We'd better talk to him,' Peter said.

Larensen was calling out again. 'Hey, professor! Professor. You meet my wife, eh? We all have a drink, then I take you on board. I fix, eh?'

'This is awful!' John said.

Peter hurried forward and spoke to Larensen. 'Shut up, or I'll hit you!'

'What for?'

'Talking in English like that – you must be crazy!'

Larensen flung his arm round Peter's neck. 'You wouldn't hit old Larensen?' He still spoke in English. 'You wouldn't hit old Larensen who helped you out of Germany?' He was maudlin now. 'That's no way to treat a pal, eh, professor?' He turned to John. 'That's no way to treat a pal, is it, professor?'

'Shut up,' Peter repeated.

'Come and have a drink,' Larensen insisted. 'All go and have a drink. This is my wife.' He chucked her under the chin with a large, dirty hand and winked at John. 'Prima, eh? I got plenty of money. All go and have a drink.'

He began to walk down the road, his wife and Sigmund supporting him.

'This is awful!' John said.

'We'd better follow them,' Peter told him. 'I expect they're going on board soon.'

'The sooner we get on board the better. I'd hate to get caught now through that chap getting drunk.'

'We'll have to keep him quiet somehow. As long as we can keep him away from the goons we're all right. We'll stay with them and keep him quiet. He scares me stiff.'

They followed the other three down the street and when Larensen turned into a café they followed him in. They all sat on a long seat in a small private room at the back of the café. It was a red plush-covered seat with broken springs and in front of the seat was an old, dark wood table with a strip of brightly coloured cloth across the centre. The room was divided from the front part of the café by a bead curtain and Peter sat with his back against the wall so that he could see through the curtain and out into the café.

If any soldiers come in and Larensen starts talking English I'll knock him out, he thought. He measured the distance to Larensen's jaw and decided on the exact spot to hit him.

A woman brought glasses of beer on a tray and Larensen spoke in English again.

'I bring my wife to England. I do one more job and then I bring my wife to England.'

'One more job?' John asked.

'Yes, one more trip. Then I take a rest.' He took a long pull at the glass of beer and leaned back on the narrow seat.

'We bring some Frenchmen next time,' Sigmund said.

'Frowg-aiters!' Larensen said. 'Goddam frowg-aiters. They got plenty guts, those fellas.'

'What do they do when they get here?' John asked.

'They try to get to England,' Sigmund said, 'to join the French army there. First they go to Sweden. I do not know what happens after they leave Denmark.'

'We get 'em out of Germany,' Larensen said. 'We feed 'em good. You boys hungry?'

'No thanks,' Peter said. He did not want Larensen to order anything. He did not want Larensen to do anything but keep quiet.

'You boys are hungry,' Larensen said. He called the woman from the front of the shop and ordered food and beer.

Peter sat drinking the beer and eating the food that the woman had brought. He felt more helpless than he had felt since they first escaped from the camp.

243

Larensen sat watching them eating, beaming with a vast proprietorial grin. 'That's right, you boys. Eat good. We have more eggs and bacon when we get back to the ship.'

'What time are we going back to the ship?' Peter asked.

'When it gets dark,' Sigmund told him. 'About six o'clock.'

'What shall we do with Larensen until then?' Larensen was talking to his wife in Danish.

'He is quite safe.'

'But it's all so open,' Peter said. 'You talk English openly in the street. We hear an explosion and you calmly tell us it's the power station. Even the band in the café at lunchtime was playing English songs.'

'The Danes have never been beaten.' Sigmund said it seriously. 'We are occupied but we are not beaten. We are combined against the Germans. They cannot arrest us all.'

'They can have a good try,' Peter said.

'No. They cannot arrest us all. They need us for our food. That is why we have the curfew at eight o'clock. There were too many Germans killed in the street at night. Denmark has not been ravaged like the rest of Europe because the Germans want our food. But Denmark is fighting. We have our traitors but not more than other countries. There are still Germans killed in the street at night.'

'It would be the same in England,' John said.

'Yes,' Sigmund agreed. 'I think it would be the same in England.'

Larensen was quiet now. He was occupied with his wife. The others ignored him, thankful for the silence.

During the afternoon Sigmund went down to the docks to arrange for their embarkation. He returned some time later with bad news.

244

'The Jerries are in the docks,' he said. 'There is special caution because of the rescue of Mr Olsen. I have been told to take you away from Copenhagen. We are to take a small boat from a village a few miles from here.'

'What shall we do with Larensen?' Peter asked. Larensen and his wife were sleeping.

'Leave him. He will be too noisy. Come, let us go.'

They left the café and walked up into the town, where Sigmund bought tickets for the electric railway and they sat silently watching the Danish countryside grow dim in the fading light.

'The place where we are going is on an island,' Sigmund told them. 'The island is approached by a bridge. On the bridge there may be a sentry. I shall not be much use because of my hand. You must deal with the sentry.'

Peter looked at John. All the time they had been escaping they had avoided violence. No escaping prisoner used violence unless he was within sight of freedom. The stake was too high.

'Shall we be sure of getting away once we reach the island?' Peter asked.

'Absolutely!' Sigmund said.

'Must we go to the island?' John asked. 'Can't the boat pick us up from the mainland?'

'That is impossible. The sentry must be silenced, otherwise he will give the alarm. We should be stopped by the patrol boats. This is the only way it can be done.'

Peter looked at John. 'How are you fixed for Commando work?'

'I did the old battle course,' John said. 'We'll manage all right. We'll pick up a couple of bricks on the way out.'

'I'd rather have a sandbag.'

'We'll use a sock,' John said. 'Fill it with earth.'

They left the train at a small wayside station and set out for the bridge. On the way they each took off one sock and filled it with gravel from the side of the road.

They walked on down the road without speaking, their feet brushing up the dead leaves as they walked, stirring the sweet odours of late autumn. From across the fields came the faint tang of burning wood and above them the last few dead leaves rustled in the light wind. Peter felt as he used to feel before flying on a raid, a mixture of fear and anticipation. This night-stalking was new to him and he did not know how he would react.

'There it is!' Sigmund said.

He had stopped dead in the road and was holding Peter by the arm. Ahead of them they could see the break in the trees where the gorge was, and the stark outline of the bridge.

'We'll creep along in the ditch,' Peter whispered.

'While you fix the sentry I will go to the boats,' Sigmund told them. 'When you have fixed him, cross the bridge and I will be waiting for you. You will see the boats on the right-hand side of the road. The other guards are at the far end of the island beyond the boats. Be silent.'

They climbed down into the ditch and crept towards the bridge, their footsteps deadened by the leaves.

When they reached the bridge they stopped. The ditch ended short of the bridge and a steel railing took its place, naked in the moonlight and without cover.

'We'll never get to the bridge without being seen,' Peter whispered.

John put his mouth close to Peter's ear. 'I'll go back along the ditch and attract his attention. I'll try to get his back to you, and you hit him.'

'O.K.'

John crept back along the ditch. When he was out of sight of the sentry he got up on to the road and walked slowly towards the bridge. He came within sight of the sentry, walking slowly in the middle of the road and staggering slightly as he walked.

'*Halt! Wer ist dort?*' It was the sentry's challenge.

'*Hilfe!*' John said, staggering and holding his hand to his side.

Peter, hiding in the ditch, saw the sentry bring his rifle to the ready, peering down the road. The sentry took a step forward. '*Wer ist dort?*' he repeated.

'*Hilfe!*' John groaned. He sank to his knees as though he were exhausted.

The sentry walked slowly towards him with his rifle, bayonet fixed, held in front of his body.

John moaned and fell forward, his hands on the ground in front of him.

The sentry was standing over him now, his back towards Peter. This is it, Peter thought. He scrambled from the ditch, slipping in the soft earth as he sprang. The sentry heard him, turned; and in that instant John threw himself at the man's knees.

The sentry raised his rifle and clubbed down at John's head as Peter's sandbag caught him across the shoulders. The sock was too big, too full of earth. It hit the sentry equally across the rim of his helmet and the collar of his coat.

Peter flung himself forward, clutching the sentry round the neck and bringing him crashing down on top of him. He wriggled like an eel, squirming out from under the German and going for his throat, to stop him crying out. He got his fingers round the man's neck, but it was a big neck, fleshy, and he could not feel the windpipe.

The German grunted and groped wildly for the revolver at his belt. Then he felt Peter's fingers at his throat and forgot the revolver, kicking hard with his three-quarter boots and clawing at Peter's face with his fingernails. He was fighting for his life now.

Peter fought in a cold fury, his whole strength going in one gigantic effort to stop the man from crying out. His fingers slipped from the sweat on the man's neck and he

247

felt him getting away. Then he was at the neck again. He felt the man's hands tearing at his face, his heels drumming on the metal of the road. He was on top of the man now, sitting astride him, his fingers on his windpipe, pressing, pressing, pressing . . .

The man's struggles grew weaker. Peter felt the body grow slack and without resistance. He sat there for some time, pressing his thumbs into the man's neck, making sure that he was unconscious. Then he relaxed. He got to his feet. His knees were trembling and his face was sore where the man's nails had gouged the flesh.

The body of the sentry was sprawled in the road, head flung at an unusual angle, mouth open as though he still struggled for breath.

John lay where he had fallen. His hair was matted with dark blood. Peter loosened his collar and lifted him to a sitting position. He took him in his arms and dragged him to the side of the road. John moaned as he put him down. Then he opened his eyes and put his hands to his head.

'What happened?'

'He hit you on the head with his rifle,' Peter said.

'Where is he?'

'Over there.'

He helped John to his feet and they walked slowly across the bridge towards the boats. Peter, quiet and shaken and still trembling at the knees.

As they left the bridge they heard a low shout; and there was Sigmund standing by one of the boats.

'It needs three of us,' he said. 'It is stuck on the mud.'

They waded into the shallow water and began to heave the boat into deep water. It scraped harshly as it slipped across the mud and they expected every minute to hear the sound of a rifle shot or the challenge of a sentry. They pushed the boat into deeper water and clambered aboard.

'I will steer,' Sigmund told them. 'You get the sail up and then lie in the bottom of the boat.'

Peter and John hoisted the sail. There was a light offshore wind which heeled the boat over as Sigmund tacked along the shore.

Peter lay in the bottom of the boat, smelling the strong smell of fish and salt water and listening to the sound of the low waves slapping against the sides. He wiped his hands on his trouser legs and tried not to think of the sentry. They would be in Sweden by the morning.

It was cold in the bottom of the boat. He shivered in his sweat-soaked clothes.

Chapter Twelve

The Welcome Home

Some weeks later, having met Phil in Sweden, they were flown to England. They landed at an airfield in the Midlands and it was raining. It was four o'clock in the morning and they were not expected.

After a delay of two hours they were taken before the station intelligence officer. He was wearing tartan trews and could not have been less interested. He took their ranks, names and numbers. The German officer who had interrogated Peter when he was captured had been more polite.

'Can we get anything to eat?' John asked.

The officer was flustered. He had been asleep when they had landed and he was not yet fully awake. 'You'll find something in the airmen's mess. I'll have you called in the morning. Your train goes at seven-thirty.'

In the airmen's mess they were given cold bacon and potatoes on enamel plates. The corporal in charge was worried because they had not brought their own knives and forks.

They found three empty beds in a crowded dormitory and fell asleep. Half an hour later Peter was awakened by a batman. 'The major wants to see you, sir.'

'But I've just seen him.'

'He told me to call you again, sir.'

Peter began to put on a dressing-gown.

'I should advise you to dress properly, sir. The major's apt to object if you're not properly dressed.'

Peter had been ordered about for so long now that he took it calmly. Soon he was standing in front of the major's desk. This time the major had a captain with him. Intelligence. Peter thought he looked a pretty dim type.

The captain asked Peter's rank, name and number.

'You've just had them.'

The major mumbled something about losing the papers. He looked too old to be up at that time of the morning. Peter felt sorry for him. He gave him his rank, name and number.

'How long were you a prisoner?' the major asked.

Peter told him.

'What was it like?' He seemed to be making conversation, making up for getting him out of bed. Peter wondered what to say. He could describe the damp barrack blocks, fetid and close from overcrowded living, the rows and rows of two-tier bunks, the scuffing of wooden clogs on damp concrete as the bearded and dirty Kriegies queued up for the midday ration of cabbage water. He could describe the circuit, the crowd of lonely figures, shoulders hunched, eyes on the ground, mooching slowly round; refusing to acknowledge the existence of the wire, self-contained figures, lonely in spite of the proximity of a thousand like them. But what could he say of the companionship, of the humour, of the fierce joy of baiting the Hun? What could he say of the home that each man had made of his bed space, the rough shelves above the beds, the few books, the photographs, the sudden generous gifts when the giver had so little to spare? Of how each man was stripped bare in front of his fellows and was accepted for what he was rather than for what he had. What could he say of the decency and humour of the average man? Words could not convey what he felt about that queer, unhappy, glorious, quarrelling, generous, indomitable, scruffy family that he had left behind.

'It wasn't so bad in some ways,' he said. 'The chaps were pretty good.'

'How did the Germans treat you?' the major asked.

He could tell of Alan, shot through the belly as he climbed the wire; starvation rations, solitary confinement, the stupid, petty restrictions. He could tell of the kindly tolerant guards with families at home and their fear of the Gestapo and the Russian front. Of the bullying braggart of a Feldwebel who was nothing but a lout and could have been born in England as easily as in Germany.

'They weren't too bad,' he said. 'There were some decent ones.'

'I hear you had a golf course,' the captain said.

A golf course . . . Peter was angry at first. He looked at the smug non-prisoner face. Golf course. He remembered the earnest ragged Kriegies knocking home-made balls round the huts with clubs made from melted-down metal water-jugs. He turned to the major.

'I'd like to turn in now, sir. We're leaving early in the morning. By the way – could you let us have any money?'

'You should have been given English money before you left Sweden,' the major aid.

'We've only got Swedish money.'

'We've no machinery for giving you English money here.' The major was getting flustered again.

There was a short silence. The intelligence captain spoke.

'Do you have a cheque book?'

'Don't be silly – we've just come from a prison camp!'

The captain turned to the major; he had solved the problem. 'I think we can trust them, sir. After all, they *are* officers.'

Glossary

Abort	(German) Latrine
Appel	(German) Roll Call
Arbeitskarte	(German) Workman's identity card
Ausweis	(German) Identity Card
Chocker	(slang) Unhappy, discontented
Cobber	(slang) Mate, friend
Cooler	Punishment cell
Dienst	(German) Service, Job
Feldwebel	(German) Non-Commissioned Officer
Gefreiter	(German) Lance-corporal
Gen	(R.A.F. slang) Information, details, news
Hauptmann	(German) Captain
Hitlerjugend –	
Hitlermädchen –	Nazi Youth Organizations
Hundmeister	(German) Dog trainer
Klim	(Milk spelt backwards) Brand of powdered milk in Red Cross parcels
Kommandantur	(German) German guards' quarters
Kriegie	Kriegsgefangener (German) Prisoner of War
Lager Offizier	(German) Compound Officer
Moling	(P.O.W. slang) Digging a tunnel and packing the earth behind you as you move forward

Oberst	(German) Colonel
Op	Operational flight over enemy territory
Posten	(German) Sentry
Schnapps	A powerful liquor
Seismograph	Instrument for recording earth tremors
Stooge	(P.O.W. slang) Person on a "Dienst"
Straflager	(German) Punishment camp
Verboten	(German) Forbidden
Völkischer Beobachter	Well-known German newspaper

Armada
Gift Classics

An attractive collection of beautifully illustrated stories, including some of the finest and most enjoyable children's stories ever written.

Some of the older, longer titles have been skilfully edited and abridged.

ARMADA

All these books are available at your local bookshop or newsagent, or can be ordered from the publisher. To order direct from the publishers just tick the title you want and fill in the form below:

Name _____

Address _____

_____

Send to: Collins Childrens Cash Sales
          PO Box 11
          Falmouth
          Cornwall
          TR10 9EN

Please enclose a cheque or postal order or debit my Visa/ Access –

   Credit card no:

   Expiry date:

   Signature:

– to the value of the cover price plus:

UK: 60p for the first book, 25p for the second book, plus 15p per copy for each additional book ordered to a maximum charge of £1.90.

BFPO: 60p for the first book, 25p for the second book plus 15p per copy for the next 7 books, thereafter 9p per book.

Overseas and Eire: £1.25 for the first book, 75p for the second book. Thereafter 28p per book.

Armada reserve the right to show new retail prices on covers which may differ from those previously advertised in the text or elswhere.

ARMADA